PRAYERS
THAT WILL MAKE HELL NERVOUS

WARFARE EDITION
VOLUME 1

CHARLINE S. AYALA

Prayers that Will Make HELL Nervous: Warfare Edition, Volume 1
by Charline S. Ayala

Cover design, editing, book layout, and publishing services by KishKnows, Inc., Richton Park, Illinois, 708-252-DOIT

admin@kishknows.com, www.kishknows.com

ISBN: 978-0-578-93405-1
LCCN: 2021911924

All rights reserved. No part of this book may be reproduced, distributed, or transmitted in any form or by any means, including photocopying, recording, digital scanning, or other electronic or mechanical methods, without the prior written permission of the publisher, except in the case of brief quotations embodied in critical reviews and certain other noncommercial uses permitted by copyright law. For permission requests, please contact Charline Ayala at AuthorCharlineAyala@gmail.com.

Some Scripture references may be paraphrased versions or illustrative references of the author. Unless otherwise specified, all other references are from the **King James Version of the Bible.**

Scriptures marked **NIV** are taken from **THE HOLY BIBLE, NEW INTERNATIONAL VERSION®, NIV®** Copyright © 1973, 1978, 1984, 2011 by Biblica, Inc.® Used by permission. All rights reserved worldwide.

Copyright © 2021 by Charline S. Ayala

Printed in the United States of America

DEDICATION

I dedicate this book to my **Abba Father**.

I thank you for bringing me out of the darkness and calling me into your marvelous light. I am forever grateful for the ultimate sacrifice you paid on the Cross that saved my soul. You are worthy of all the glory. Thank you, Jesus.

I dedicate this book to my stepmother, **Huong Dang**. May your beautiful soul rest in peace. You always had the biggest dreams for me; some were realistic, and some were just outrageous…but all you ever wanted was to see me succeed. I thank you for never giving up on me and for believing in me wholeheartedly. You always showed me the best parts of life. Your laugh was so contagious that I can still hear it today. Thank you for the special events where you celebrated me in every way. Since I was a child, you were there for every moment of my life; and I hold you so dear to my heart, because you never missed a moment to tell me or show me how much you loved me. I wish you could see this book be released…but since the Lord has called you to join Him, I dedicate this to you, my beautiful Queen.

TABLE OF CONTENTS

Dedication	iii
Preface	vii
Introduction	xv

SPIRITUAL ADVANCEMENT

Spiritual Advancement Testimony	3
Baptism in the Holy Spirit	13
Welcome the Holy Spirit	17
Spiritual Advancement	21
Accuracy in the Spirit	25

SPIRITUAL WARFARE

Spiritual Warfare Testimony	31
Reverse the Curse	49
Deliverance Declaration	53
Soul Tie Sever	57
Victory over Fear	61

PROTECTION

Protection Testimony	67
Divine Protection	79
Protection over Family	83
Protection over the Nations	87
Protection from Illnesses and Diseases	93
About the Author	97
Acknowledgments	99

PREFACE

WHAT IS SPIRITUAL WARFARE?

Spiritual warfare is a battle against the evil forces, spirits, and demons in the unseen world that interfere with a person's way of life.

> *"For our battle is not against flesh and blood, but against principalities, against powers, against the rulers of the darkness of this world, against spiritual wickedness in high places."*
> ***(Ephesians 6:12 KJV)***

Ultimately, what this means is that there is a spiritual war going on between good and evil. These spiritual forces are here on a wicked mission to separate us from our Heavenly Father.

My church home, D3 Ministries, hosted a strategic leadership training workshop where we hosted the amazing Pastor Vondell Robinson, who was invited to teach on spiritual warfare. What he said blew my mind. He stated, *"**Spiritual warfare** is resisting or overcoming and defeating the enemy's lies when he comes in the form of temptation, accusations, or deception. Then there's **deliverance**, which deals with demonic bondage and being set free from everything inside of you that doesn't mirror Christ."*

There are many different levels to spiritual warfare; but before I can go into the depths of what Satan is cooking up in the unseen world, we first have to acknowledge that we live in a spiritual world, not just a physical one. We are living in a world where the enemy isn't playing fair…he is playing for keeps. He is fighting to keep our *souls*…and some of us haven't yet come to fully understand the power that lies within us as a child of God. The Scriptures say, *"Greater is he that is in me than he who is in the world."* **(1 John 4:4)** Therefore, because of who we are in Christ, we carry the power to stand against the devious and manipulative plans of the devil.

How do we activate that power? Through prayer, worship, reading the Holy Book, and intimacy with the precious Holy Spirit. The hits that hurt the most are the ones that we don't see coming, but prayer equips us for the attacks.

Through prayer, God will reveal the attacks to us before they even come, because He wants us to be prepared to fight back. Another way to tap into the power of God is through fasting. Fasting is necessary because it disciplines our flesh. When we give our flesh what it wants, it will strip us of our spiritual power, so we need to ask ourselves what we are feeding…our flesh or our spirit? That which we give power to is what we choose to feed. So, if you are someone like me who wants to bust the enemy upside his head, your weapons for warfare are worship, fasting, prayer, reading, meditating on the Scriptures, and intimacy with your helper, the Holy Spirit.

I've experienced a high level of spiritual warfare in this walk; but at some point, I had to realize the power that lives within me and stop giving the enemy the keys to my life. It was time to evict him and take my keys back, knowing the power that lives within me as the Bride of Christ.

Although at times we can be self-centered, the truth of the matter is that this is bigger than us—our entire nation is under attack. It amazes me how everyone gets into an uproar when they hear that our country is at war…as if we haven't been at war all of our lives. Since the day we were born, we have been fighting for our lives against the enemy, who is like *"a roaring lion seeking whom he may devour"* **(1 Peter 5:8 KJV)**. I am sorry to be the deliverer of bad news; but like the pervert that he is, he has been lusting after the children of God since the day we took our first breath. If you have not already guessed who this mysterious enemy is that I speak of, it is Satan and his little army of demons and devils. I say "little" because I really despise him; but I don't *sleep on him* (don't get deceived) because the enemy is cunning and powerful. Granted he is nowhere near as mighty and powerful as the Lord, but we give the enemy power every time we participate in evil and wicked deeds. It is as if we give the enemy the key to causing chaos and destruction in our lives.

What I'm saying is that we cannot play with the devil; we cannot play with sin. If we leave any doors open for the enemy to come in through sin, ungodly living, or disbelief, then we can potentially lose our mind, our family, and even our life. What's even worse is that our sins don't just affect us; they also have the potential to become a generational curse if we are not careful.

For those who may not know him well, the devil is a liar, a murderer, a sower of discord, and an adversary. He is wicked, evil, a thief, prideful, aggressive, a pervert, and a destroyer. Pretty much sounds like the world we are living in now, so I guess it should not be that hard to tell that Satan has been ruling the earth for many years. The good news is that when Christ died on the Cross, the devil was defeated! Christ defeated death (the enemy) the "first" time when He died on the Cross for our sins. If you are looking forward to your ticket into the kingdom of heaven, you must receive salvation and be born again through Christ to be saved from the "second" death (judgment) when He returns. Christ gave us hope. The problem is that we have to live with this conniving demon until Christ returns, and Satan is making it his business to drag down as many souls as he can before that day comes. God knew that we didn't stand a chance in this world filled with sin, which is exactly why we need Christ.

> *"For God so loved the world, that he gave his only begotten Son, that whosoever believeth in him should not perish, but have everlasting life."* ***(John 3:16 KJV)***

Many people wonder why the devil is still wreaking havoc in our lives if he has already been defeated. Why would God cast him down and leave him here on earth among His beloved children? I've heard many questions pertaining to why God does things and allows things to happen. My faith says I'm sure God the Father has a reasonable explanation for everything He does so I won't question Him, especially since that the devil cannot do anything without consulting God first. Even demons believe in the name of Jesus, and they tremble at the mention of His name ***(James 2:19)***.

I believe that the devil is probably necessary for the many testimonies that have to come forth so that God can get the glory out of how we overcame everything that the enemy meant for evil. I believe he may be here to provoke people and bring them to their lowest point so that they run into the loving arms of Christ, just as I did. Maybe he is here so that the Lord can prepare a table for us in the presence of our enemies, and the enemy can watch us take our place as worshipers of Christ. God is creative and full of mysteries.

I haven't received the full revelation as to why the enemy has any right to cause destruction in the world or in our lives; but God is intentional, and I would say from experience that I know God didn't just leave us for dead. He gave us authority and dominion over the earth just as He did to Adam; and with that authority, we are able to stop every plan, plot, and ploy of the enemy. Through our prayers and intercession, we are able to release God's hand to manifest here on earth and release His miracles, signs, and wonders. Through righteous living, we are able to shut every door to the enemy, giving him no access into our lives…and through reading the Bible, we are able to use the Word of God to combat the enemy in warfare, just as Jesus did when He was in the wilderness and said, *"It is written…get thee behind me…"* Words are powerful…but the *Word of God* is our weapon against the pits of hell.

Many of our daily struggles come from demonic spirits working behind the scenes; some are generational, some are through sins we have participated in, and some are just because we are loved by God.

If you struggle with being a *pathological liar*, there is a spirit operating behind that. If you struggle with *violence* and *have thoughts of murdering people*, there is a spirit operating behind that. If you struggle with *evil thoughts, a wicked imagination,* and *unclean desires*, there is a spirit operating behind that. If you struggle with *gossip* and *causing division among people*, there is a spirit operating behind that.

If you are *prideful, aggressive, confused, jealous, depressed, sick,* or *living in fear*, there are demonic spirits at work. If you struggle with *addiction, confused sexuality, adultery, prostitution, incest,* or *perversion,* and are struggling with *believing in Christ and the antichrist*, there are spirits operating behind all of that!

Don't be alarmed. May I say, the devil is a liar. You are not crazy, depressed, or a bad person…literally everything that we struggle with has some kind of spirit behind it, whether good or bad, simply because this is a spiritual world, and we are spiritual beings having human experiences. For those still in the struggle, know that the hope is in knowing the greater the struggle, the greater the calling.

As we are living in the last days, this is not a time to lose hope, because Christ has given us everything that we need to show us how to live and stand up to Satan and his army. In order to do this, we must trust in God and leave no room for the enemy, or he will have a *field day* with us (take advantage); and before we know it, we will be holding on to our lives by a thread. Take it from me. I am no stranger to Satan and his works…in fact, I've danced with the devil a few times. We went on a few dates, and he was my little *sugar daddy* for a time—but that relationship came to an end when he stabbed me in the back, used me, and abused me, then chewed me up and spit me out.

Yep, just like any no-good ex-boyfriend, he will mask himself as Prince Charming. He wines and dines you; then when he is through with you, he will use you and abuse you and then move on to the next available vessel. I am no one you can just use and abuse, so now I'm on an assignment to destroy the kingdom of darkness by shining light on all its evil works and influences and bringing many souls back to Christ through this book full of testimonies, worship, praise, and prayers.

You might notice in this book that the prayers are structured. This is not because I believe that prayer should be so structured that it doesn't give room for the Holy Spirit to change your direction; but because each time I pray, I love to start off with praising the Lord for who He is and what He has done, then repenting of my wrongdoings, asking God to cleanse me and renew a right spirit within me, asking Him for what I need, presenting my requests to Him, and thanking Him for what I'm believing Him for as if I have already received it. Then I declare His Word so it will be established.

As you continue to pray, you may be led differently. I encourage you to follow the leading of the Holy Spirit, but you can use this method as a guide to assist you in covering everything in your prayers.

One last word: With new *levels*, there will be new *devils*. As you go forth in this book, warfare is to be expected…so put on the armor of God and get ready for battle, because Satan is not going to let you go out without a fight. I don't know about you…but the devil is *not* about to come for *my* family, *my* finances, *my* health, and *my* mind. I'm coming back with fire to tear down the kingdom of hell!

> It's time you take back the authority and dominion that the devil stole from you, and get ready to Make. Hell. Nervous.

INTRODUCTION

My name is Charline Ayala, and I am from Crown Heights in Brooklyn, New York. My mother's side of the family is from Ceiba, Puerto Rico, and my father's side of the family are American and Trinidadian, which makes me American, Puerto Rican, and Trinidadian. I was also very fortunate to be raised in an Asian household with my stepmother Huong, who was Vietnamese. The benefits of being multicultural has played a major role in who I am today.

Unfortunately, growing up for me was far from a walk in the park, as my childhood was stolen from me before I even entered into this world. As a small child, I was faced with many afflictions in my life, and I just didn't see a way out. Faced with rejection, I began looking for love in all the wrong places, which led me down a path of destruction. I thought death was the only option left…until the day Jesus revealed Himself to me. I ran to the altar, and He wrapped His loving arms around me and sang me a love song. On August 20, 2019, I gave my life to back to Christ. Since that day, my life has never been the same.

I have written this book to assist you in your prayer life, combat warfare, and unleash the prayer warrior within you. I am sharing many aspects of my personal testimony to encourage you, as well as to give God the glory for helping me overcome rejection, unforgiveness, unbelief, sickness, weakness, divorce, rage, fear, abuse, warfare, strongholds, suicidal thoughts and actions, molestation, bisexuality, pornography, bipolar disorder, schizophrenia, New Age spirituality, witchcraft, and many other generational curses. My forever thoughts were, *"Nobody loves me," "I'm not good enough," "I'm a terrible person,"* and *"I deserve to die."* You couldn't convince me that I had a purpose in life because my mind was stuck in its ways. It was not by might, not by power, but by His spirit and the blood of the Lamb that I have overcome a life of sin and death.

NOTHING BUT GOD.

God took what Satan intended for evil and turned it around to use for His good and His glory. He showed me that there is purpose on the inside of me. He said that I will live and not die. He said I am the head and not the tail, above only and not beneath, the lender and not the borrower. I am the generational curse breaker. He said that my bloodline will be restored.

> I am *healed*. I am *accepted*.
> I am *beautiful*. I am *treasured*.
> I am *fearless*, *bold*, and *courageous*.
> I am a *masterpiece*.
> I am *chosen*…and
> ***I am*** *who* ***God*** *says I am!*

Prayer is not a hobby for me. It's a *lifestyle*. I am the only one in my immediate family who is saved, so I am carrying the weight of my bloodline on my shoulders, interceding for them until they are saved. Their souls are attached to *my* "yes" and to *my* obedience. Through prayer, I am believing God to redeem my family; and just like myself, there are many generational curse breakers out there that God is looking to work through.

Through prayer, we release the hand of God to manifest here on earth and in our lives. Prayer changes things. Words change worlds… and *His Word* is our mighty weapon in warfare. I enjoyed writing this book because my desire is to see others set free from the hands of the enemy and to see them prospering in the things of God. I know that if Christ can take someone like me who was rebellious and loved to play with sin, and still use me to effect change in the atmosphere and in people's lives, then *He can do the same for you.*

This book includes fervent prayers that are lengthy, simply because it encourages you to spend more time in God's presence, and target the areas that the enemy uses to keep us in bondage. I didn't just want to write a whole bunch of prayers without testifying about how these very prayers were answered in my own life. With each chapter, you can expect to read a testimony of how God has moved on my behalf for the very thing you may be believing Him for, and you can look forward to reading about the good, the bad, and the ugly truth along the way. God has brought me so far from where I once was. I am an open book, and I am unashamed of what I've been through…therefore, I have laid down my life on these pages. I choose to be an open scroll as you experience the deep parts of my life firsthand. As you read these prayers and expect *your* prayers to be answered, know that the enemy will not be happy about it…so tighten up your armor, pick up your sword…and be who God has called you to be!

Know that if you're still alive, it's because you have purpose on the inside of you. The more you pray the will of the Father, the more your heart will align with His heart. When your hearts become intertwined, you will be able to see yourself the way He sees you… and when you begin to see yourself how God sees you, *nothing in the world can convince you otherwise.* Walk in your destiny, knowing greater is He that is in you then He that is in the world *(1 John 4:4 KJV, paraphrased).* Don't give up, because God isn't done with you. It's not over, so consider yourself victorious! The devil is defeated, and the victory is won. Give Him praise, and remember that the ultimate victory belongs to Jesus Christ of Nazareth.

OPENING PRAYER

"The effectual fervent prayer of a righteous man availeth much."
(James 5:16 KJV)

Before you begin reading, I want to pray with you…

Heavenly Father, I thank you for the life of this person who, by no coincidence, purchased this book. Lord, usher in the presence of your Holy Spirit as they read. The ultimate price you paid on the Cross was a true love story, so we exalt thee.

Lord, release your spirit and agape love to flow through the words on these pages. Let the reader begin to feel your presence manifest.

Reader, I decree that chains will begin to fall off of your life right now, because you chose to come to Christ. I decree that the veil that has been keeping you from seeing the gospel is being lifted up right now, in the name of Jesus. I decree and declare that the smoke screen that clouds your vision is being cleared right now, and you will begin to see with 20/20 vision into the spirit realms. I release angels wherever you are, to war in the spirit on your behalf by placing explosive charges in strategic places to destroy every stronghold in your life. I bind all of Satan's power over your life, and I declare that Satan must shut up…as you pray these prayers, he will no longer have the power to speak to you or influence you any longer.

I bind up all of the evil forces that are lingering around you, and I declare they are out of service and no longer able to operate in your life. I cancel every assignment of the enemy that he has attached to your life. I shut every door that you have given the enemy access to in your heart, soul, and mind. Using the authority God has given me, I break the headship of the serpent in your life. I speak that God will begin to heal all the pain in your heart that stops you from moving into the destiny that the Lord has ordained for you. I decree that you will be filled with knowledge of the Father's will and grow in the knowledge of who He is through all the wisdom and understanding that His spirit gives.

As you read the prayers that I have written, I pray that the Lord will help you live a life worthy to Him, and that your obedience will please Him in every way. I pray that you will begin to bear good fruit in every good work. I pray that you will be strengthened by the power of God according to His glorious might. Even in the midst of weakness, may the Lord give you great endurance and patience to press toward the mark. I pray that the Lord will give you fruit-producing revelation to know Christ better, and that the eyes of your heart will be opened and enlightened. I pray that the Lord will release His spiritual power through revelation, so that you may see the glory of Christ.

I come into agreement with your faith, so that the Lord will begin to release His Dunamis power to take back control of your life. I pray that you will walk with a hedge of protection everywhere that you step. I pray that you will begin to have dreams and visions, and that angels will be sent to minister to you about your purpose.

I pray that you will walk in the full armor of God, so that you may stand against the wiles of the devil. May these weapons destroy every proud argument and spirit of rebellion against God. I pray that you will begin to demolish every wall that can be built to keep you from finding Christ, and that He will arrest your heart and bring you back to Himself every time you stray away. In the name of Jesus, I pray that the Lord will begin to change your heart, so that your desires will become His desires as you give your obedience to Christ. I pray that the Holy Spirit will hover over you and protect you, and that you will be shielded in favor wherever you go. I pray that godly people will be put in your path every day. I declare that the spirit of freedom, liberty, truth, and life is your portion, in the mighty name of Jesus.

> *Father, I ask that you bless the reader, and show them your mighty miracles as they decree and declare your Word over their lives. Thank you for rescuing them from the dominion of darkness. Thank you for forgiving their sins and bringing forth redemption. Thank you for always keeping your promises, for He who began a good work will bring it to completion at the day of Jesus Christ.* **(Philippians 1:6 KJV**, *paraphrased*)

> *Lord, if it's aligned with your will, create from them a "power-punching-stick-of-dynamite" prayer warrior. I decree that Satan will hate their roar, and hell will be nervous; but the heavens will rejoice at the mention of your name. Give them their hearts' desire, and unleash the prayer warrior within.*

I seal this prayer in Jesus' matchless name. Amen.

SPIRITUAL ADVANCEMENT

SPIRITUAL ADVANCEMENT TESTIMONY

Coming to the understanding that the spiritual world is actually more real than the natural may seem crazy to some; but for me, it was normal. From childhood, I had many supernatural experiences; and even in my adult life, I've experienced some supernatural and paranormal events. I truly believe there are levels to this, because I remember when I saw the world one way; and the next day, my world was never the same. It's almost as if the world you once knew is completely gone, and you enter into this new world where everything and everyone is operating behind some kind of spirit. I guess some people would call it going through the "matrix" or being "woke."

Once I went through the "matrix," I literally felt different about everything. My desires changed, my whole perspective on life changed, and my relationships with the people around me changed. Then, strangely, this anger began to build up on the inside of me for everyone around me that I felt was "asleep." I would call them "zombies," because they were not "awake." In other words, they were still living by what they saw and not acknowledging the unseen. I became obsessed with the universe, horoscopes, numerology, government conspiracies, and New Age spirituality. Oh, and don't get me started about the laws of attraction. After reciting many affirmations and reading *The Secret*, I became a "master of manifesting." If I wanted it, I got it. If I said it, I saw it. If I thought it, it came to me. God forbid you made me angry...I've manifested car accidents, financial problems, and anything I could think of to make you have a bad day. I was a negative force to be reckoned with.

I was so great at manifesting that I felt like I was God Himself. As a matter a fact, that's exactly how I referred to myself. *"I am God."* I couldn't see God for myself, nor hear Him or feel Him, so it only made sense to me that with all my new "powers," I was my own god the whole time. I was so in tune with the universe. I found a new love for nature and saw it differently...I just wanted to sit with the trees and smell the grass while I watched videos on how to activate my third eye and learn about chakras. I become very sensitive to people's energies and feelings. My intuition was so accurate, it was scary. I was able to feel everyone's emotions and became extra aware of everything around me. I swore up and down I was a mind reader because of the way I was able to predict people's thoughts and knew what was about to happen before it happened. I felt "enlightened" and "illuminated." It was surreal.

I thought I was so "woke," but little did I know that I was blinded by the enemy, and his little demons and devils were operating behind every lie I was believing. You call it "woke," but I call it *deception*. The enemy put a veil over my eyes, and I could only see what he wanted me to see and believe what he wanted me to believe. But let me shine some light on Satan's deception. You are not truly "woke" until you come to know the truth, the gospel of Jesus Christ. Everything outside of the gospel is a lie. I am a living witness; my whole world changed the day I encountered the Holy Spirit and heard the heavenly language of speaking in tongues.

Here's how it all started. After realizing how far down the rabbit hole I had fallen, I reached out to an old coworker of mine, Michael Logan, and he invited me to his church. Although I grew up in the church, I had lost my faith along the way, and I didn't believe in the gospel of Jesus at the time. I believed I was my own god; but at this point on the path of destruction I was traveling, I thought, *"Let's try this Jesus thing."* What did I have to lose? My good friend Mike, along with his wife Kelly, picked me up from my house in New Jersey. As I got in the car, my body began to tremble, especially because the night before, I had some drinks with my friends, and I was on my way to church with a hangover. As we were driving to the church, I had so many questions, and Mike had so many vague answers. The anticipation was building the whole way there; and although I was nervous in the flesh, my spirit was settled. It was like my spirit knew that Jesus had called me…and it was time to meet my Savior.

After about a thirty-minute drive, we finally arrived at the church in Highbridge, located in the Bronx. We got out of the car and walked towards the church; and as I walked through the doors, I didn't know what to think except *"Okay. We are here. There's no turning back, so let's see what happens."* I took a seat and waited for the service to start. As I was sitting down, I began looking around everywhere by habit; and when I turned my head back around in front of me, there was an utterance coming from the mouth of this woman of God. I was so intrigued by the sound that I started staring at her, trying to figure out what island she was from and what language she was speaking. I knew it was a language that I had never heard before, and I was thinking to myself *"What kind of witchcraft is this?"*

She looked so focused, and I couldn't keep my eyes off of her. I didn't know what I was about to get myself into, but I didn't feel the urge to leave, so I sat patiently until it was time.

The service began, and the worshipers sang these beautiful, sweet songs of worship. Someone call a plumber because my eyes started leaking. I couldn't contain the tears as they started flowing down my face. More and more tears began to fall; and the next thing I knew, I was drowning in my tears as I felt a presence come over me that I had never felt before. Pastor Ruth, who is now my spiritual mom, began to sing, and she stopped as she pointed me out and said, *"I see a light shining over you, and there are angels all around you."* I thought she was a little crazy because I couldn't see any angels—all I could see was strangers surrounding me—but her voice was so beautiful, and the presence of God was so strong that I just stood there and wept harder and harder.

I didn't know anybody around me, but I felt so much love in the atmosphere. They wrapped a white sheet around me and written on it in big, bold red letters was "JESUS." I held that sheet so tightly that I felt like Jesus Himself was hugging me and comforting me throughout the service.

After an intense worship time, I pulled myself together enough to get through the rest of the service…until it was time for the altar call. I wanted to go up to the altar, but I was so nervous. I brought Kelly with me, and she stood with me holding my hand every step of the way. I got to the front of the altar; and as I was standing there, the pastor began to pray over me—and there it was again, the same language that I had heard before. This time, the power and fire behind it shifted something in my whole spirit.

Something came over me. My body began to shake, and I dropped to the floor. My eyes were closed, and all I heard were voices praying over me. They began to speak to me about things that only

God would know. I felt an intense pain in my stomach, like I was being tortured. I was crying, kicking, and screaming. I just wanted it to be over. I went through a whole deliverance.

The screaming finally stopped—there was a release; and at that very instant, I felt a huge weight lifted off of my shoulders. I knew at that moment that God was real, and I went right back up to the altar to give my life to Christ. I went home, and my mind was racing with thoughts and questions. All I could think about were the utterances coming from their mouths, and the things that they had known about my life. What was that feeling that had come over me? Why was I screaming like that? I had every who, what, and how in my mind, and the only answer I knew for a fact was that JESUS IS REAL…and that everything I believed before Him was a lie.

From that moment on, I knew that I wanted more of whatever that feeling was. I had many questions that needed to be answered, so I started attending the church faithfully and joined the discipleship class. I came to find out that the beautiful language I was hearing was the evidence of speaking in tongues. The screaming was because I was going through a deliverance, getting rid of the tormenting spirits that were torturing me. And I found out that Pastor Ruth wasn't crazy…she was just very prophetic…a prophet of God. With all the love and support I received after joining the church, I knew I was exactly where I belonged.

God is so intentional. He knew just how to get and keep my attention. The logo for the church had fire in it, and He knew how much I loved to play with fire. (Literally. I was lowkey a pyromaniac.) I used to stare at the banner with the logo of fire and feel empowered every time. There was truly a "Holy Ghost Fire" coming out of this church, and I was intrigued.

After becoming acclimated to the church, the enemy showed up and started triggering some old feelings in me. I started to feel a little jealous being around my brothers and sisters in Christ, because they were able to speak in tongues, and I was not. I began to believe and asked God for the evidence of speaking in tongues. I asked Him for it consistently for two months straight, and I didn't get it. And many times, I felt like giving up, thinking maybe I just wasn't meant to have it.

That was a spirit of discouragement trying to stop me; but those who know me know that I won't stop until I get what I want, so I called my pastor, Ruth Langhorn, and expressed my feelings to her about wanting to speak in tongues. She sent me the Scripture passage ***1 Corinthians 14:1-5***. I began to read this Scripture every day and continued to ask God for the baptism of the Holy Spirit. Slowly but surely, I began to hear the sounds of the utterance in my head, but I thought I was just making it up or that I was delusional. I thought I was faking it, and here came that spirit of discouragement again. I called Pastor Ruth again, sharing with her my experiences of hearing the sounds in my head. She said, *"Open your mouth and speak, and begin to thank God over and over."* Okay, so here I am. I'm over here like *"Umm, okay,"* standing in my room, staring out of my window, hoping that Jesus sees how hard I'm trying. I open my mouth like *"Ahh thank you, Jesus, thank you, Jesus,"* over and over. The spirit of discouragement showed up again and brought some friends with him named guilt, shame, and unbelief.

Despite the mental warfare, the warrior in me just wouldn't give up, so I kept at it. I was consistent with it, talking to the Lord in the shower, *"Ahh Lord, she told me to open my mouth. It's open, Lord. Let it come out of my mouth like water, because I don't think it sounds like this in my head—it's not right."* I called Pastor Ruth again and said, *"I don't think I'm doing this right,"* and she explained to me, *"It's like a newborn baby learning their first words. It starts off small; and gradually, you will begin to speak. It will sound funny at first, but don't worry about how it sounds. Stop trying to control it, and let God do it."*

With the amazing guidance from my pastor, my faith increased, and I began hearing the utterance in my head more and more. It had been three whole months since I was saved, and I had been praying. I heard it in my head and then I began to babble little words, but still nothing major. After an event we had in the church, I pulled my pastor to the side and said, *"Okay, I think I got it."*

I took a leap of faith and started speaking the little mumbled words that I had been hearing. I was so embarrassed because I thought I sounded crazy and was making it up in my head. She covered my ears, removing all distractions, and said, *"Speak."* I began to speak, and it started to flow, and my language started to change. I felt like I had graduated from a baby to a preteen. I couldn't believe I was doing it! I was actually speaking; but there was a part of me that was resisting so I kept holding myself back, because in my mind I still thought I was making it up.

A week or two later, I was officially baptized with the Holy Spirit. I was speaking in my heavenly language, and it was flowing out like water. It was a liberating feeling…something I had never felt before in my life. I began to speak nonstop until it become natural to me, and I was so excited.

As a maturing Christian, I must inform you that being baptized in the Holy Spirit is so much more than just speaking in tongues. The Holy Spirit is a person who is your helper, a paraclete, wisdom, understanding, council, fortitude, knowledge, a healer, and most importantly, your *friend*. Speaking in tongues is a heavenly language used to speak the mysteries of God, while the Holy Spirit helps you intercede. He lives within us. He convicts us of our sins, teaches us, guides us into all truth, reminds us, bears fruit within us, comforts us, and equips us. He is our very source of power. Having the Holy Spirit dwell on the inside of you is a gift and an unmerited blessing.

Experiencing the Holy Spirit, I now have a mediator between me and Christ. Even when I don't know the words to pray, the Holy Spirit knows exactly what I need, and how I feel, and He prays on my behalf. He has helped me intercede for others by revealing to me through His voice or through dreams and visions of the very thing I need to pray for. He's also been an amazing stylist. There have been times when I didn't know what to wear, and He put together an outfit for me…and *BAM!* Here I dripped in glory.

There have been times when I was lost on my path, and He has guided me back home with no GPS as I yielded myself to His leading. I've misplaced items, and He reminded me where I put the very thing I lost. During times when I've been brokenhearted, I would ask Him to hold me at night; and He was right there, comforting me. He has also empowered the anointing in me to fulfill the will of God.

My experiences with the Holy Spirit were the very promises that were mentioned in *John 14:26*, *Matthew 10:19-20*, *Luke 12:12*, *1 John 2:27*, *1 Corinthians 2:10*, and *John 16:13*.

I've been blessed to have encountered the Holy Spirit in many different ways. He is the source in my spiritual advancement as far as what He has already done, and the many other things He will do. He has shown me that He has my best intentions at heart. He shows willfulness and discretion, communicates the will of God, and has given me the unconditional love that I have always needed. I feel even more empowered knowing I have a relationship with the Holy Spirit and knowing that God lives in me. *"For greater is he who is in me than he who is in the world." (**1 John 4:4 KJV**, paraphrased)*

I don't have to depend on "nothing or no one," because I have the Holy Spirit! I do have other spiritual desires that I want to advance in, such as translating tongues and interpreting dreams, the gift of miracles, the gift of faith, the gift of healing, the gift of prophecy, and the gift of discerning spirits, wisdom, and knowledge—but Lord is still equipping me at this time. Spiritual advancement is a process, but I stay grounded, knowing it is more important to have a relationship with the Holy Spirit than to desire what He can do for you. Coming from not believing in the gospel, after witnessing the power of the Holy Spirit and developing an intimate love relationship with Christ, I am ever so grateful to have the Holy Spirit in my life, who is advancing me further into the kingdom of God like never before.

BAPTISM IN THE HOLY SPIRIT

"Follow the way of love and eagerly desire gifts of the spirit, especially prophecy. For anyone who speaks in a tongue does not speak to people but to God. Indeed, no one understands them; they utter mysteries by the spirit. But one who prophesies speaks to people for strengthening, encouraging, and comfort. Anyone who speaks in a tongue edifies themselves, but the one who prophesies edifies the church. I would like every one of you to speak in tongues, but I would rather have you prophesy. The one who prophesies is greater than the one who speaks in tongues, unless someone interprets, so that the church may be edified."
(1 Corinthians 14:1-5 NIV)

SHEKINAH *(EXODUS 40:35)*

You are the God who sits on the glorious throne. I am in total awe of the glory of your majestic presence. I glorify the Passover Lamb who is complete and without blemish. I magnify you, the God of light, because you know what lies in the darkness. You are my light and my salvation. From the rising to the setting sun, I will lift up your name.

You are perfect in all of your ways; I adore the Lord in holy attire. I praise you because you are a personal God, who gives me the unmerited honor of knowing who you are through your precious spirit.

Father, forgive me for participating in acts of rebellion and disobedience and for any other sins that have grieved you. If there is anything dwelling in my temple that isn't pleasing to you, I invite you to burn it by the fire of your Holy Spirit, and make room for your spirit to dwell inside of me. Send the same spirit to heal the areas in my life where you desire to bring healing, as I submit to your Holy Spirit for deliverance.

I understand that no one can receive the Holy Spirit without accepting Jesus Christ as Lord. I turn away from all rebellion and disobedience, and I choose to follow Jesus. I confess that I am a sinner, and I come to you, asking that you be the Lord over my life. I believe in my heart that Jesus died for me and rose for me, and I confess with my mouth that Jesus Christ is my Lord and Savior. I am now reborn; I am a Christian, and a child of the Almighty God.

> *"If you then, though you are evil, know how to give good gifts to your children, how much more will your Father in heaven give the Holy Spirit to those who ask him!"* **(Luke 11:13 NIV)**

Lord, I come to you, asking you to please baptize me with your Holy Spirit as you did the disciples on the Day of Pentecost. I desire to know you on a personal level, and I yearn to walk with you more deeply all the days of my life. Paul said, *"I wish you all spoke with tongues,"* according to **1 Corinthians 14:5**. As I praise your holy name and give you thanks, fill me with your Holy Spirit, giving me the evidence of speaking in tongues as you give me the utterance.

Stir up and activate the gifts of your spirit to come alive in me. As the Word of God says, *"And these signs will follow those believing these things, in Jesus' name will drive out demons and speak with new tongues…praying always with all kinds of prayer and supplication in the Spirit."* (**Mark 16:17** and **Ephesians 6:18 NIV**) I believe that I have already received what I asked for through prayer, releasing the hand of God to manifest in my life. Impart the gifts of prophecy in me, so that I may edify the church through your leadership.

Holy Spirit, I desire a covenant relationship with you through Christ Jesus. I welcome you to be my best friend, my helper, my guide, my comforter, and much more. Upon receiving the Holy Spirit, I ask that you increase my prayer life to help me maintain the fullness of the Holy Spirit. As I begin to pray in tongues, yielding myself to you, strengthen me and lead me as I intercede according to your will. As I yield myself to your Spirit, reveal the Father to me; His purposes and His ways, so that I may live a God-centered life.

Father, I understand that I cannot live a life pleasing to you without the help of the Holy Spirit. I acknowledge that my disobedience quenches the Holy Spirit; therefore, bless me with supernatural self-control and obedience to assist me in my walk, so that I will never grieve the Holy Spirit. Your Word says, *"But ye shall receive power, after that the Holy Ghost is come upon you."* **(Acts 1:8 KJV)** Empower me to be an effective servant that will profit your kingdom at all times, bringing glory to your name. Let your Holy Spirit teach and guide me into all righteousness, so that I can please you well in serving you.

Through the power of your Holy Spirit, assist me in effectively evangelizing the gospel. Give me a submissive spirit to yield to the leadership of the Holy Spirit. Let your Spirit enable me to be a positive influence in other people's lives, while encouraging and empowering them. Humble me to demonstrate my spiritual gifts in a way that will benefit both believers and non-believers. Teach me how to use my gifts to prosper in your kingdom.

For the many lost souls who have not yet come to know you, make me a living, walking testimony through the guidance of your Holy Spirit.

Thank you for a new wind and a fresh fire. Thank you for allowing me to know you through the Holy Spirit. Thank you for being omnipresent and omnipotent. Thank you, Holy Spirit, for dwelling on the inside of me.

I decree and declare that greater is He who is in me than He who is in the world. I decree and declare that I submit to the guidance of the Holy Spirit. I decree and declare that by the power of the Holy Spirit, I will live a victorious life on earth.

I seal this declaration in the blood of the Lamb, and I pray all of this in the matchless name of Jesus. Amen.

WELCOME THE HOLY SPIRIT

"Jesus said to her, 'Did I not say to you that if you would believe you would see the glory of God?'"
(John 11:40 NIV)

ELOHAY MIKAROV (JEREMIAH 23:23)

You are the radiance of the glory of God, and the exact imprint of His nature; you uphold the universe by the power of your Word. After making purification for sin, you sit at the right hand of the Majesty. You are the God who is near. Your eyes are always watching, and your ears are always listening. Holy Spirit, I welcome you into my home; saturate the atmosphere with your presence.

You are the vine; I am the branch. I remain in you, so that I may bear much fruit. Apart from you, I can do nothing…I *am* nothing. For me, it is good to be near you; I earnestly seek your face with my whole heart and soul. For in your presence, there is fullness of joy and at your right hand are pleasures forevermore. My soul pants for you; my soul thirsts to be in the presence of the Living God. You are exalted among the nations; you are exalted on earth. Keep me still, knowing that you are God and God alone. Increase my faith so I may see the full manifestation of your presence. I yearn for the courts of the Lord.

Father, forgive me for forsaking your presence. Forgive my impure heart and double-mindedness. I repent of the distractions in my life that have taken me away from your presence. I repent for any personal idols that have taken me away from having you and knowing you. I repent for giving more of my time and attention to relationships, places, materials, careers, food, sports, and possessions. Remove all distractions and take away any "lukewarmness" in my heart. Blessed are those who are pure in heart, for they shall see God. I come to you with a sincere heart in need of purification and a steadfast spirit. With the full assurance that faith brings, sprinkle my heart clean from a guilty conscience. By the power of your Holy Spirit, help me to put you above all my desires. Set me on fire for you, and ignite a flame in my heart to rekindle my love relationship with you.

Lord, you are omnipresent; where can I go from your Spirit? Or where can I flee from your presence? I invite you into my sanctuary; overwhelm my home with your Spirit. Visit me, and make your presence known in my life. Help me to prepare my heart and mind for your spirit. I welcome you to reveal yourself through your many miracles, signs, and wonders. Overwhelm my space in a way that covers me in your love. Reveal yourself to me as you did to Moses, through a blazing fire from the midst of a bush. Tell me the great unsearchable and unthinkable things that I do not know. Invite me into your dwelling place where it is so lovely, and I can find my rest. Open my understanding to your mysteries, and shine your face on me, trusting me with your secrets. Hear my voice when I call, oh Lord; I want to dwell in your house and gaze upon your beauty. Manifest your power like a spiritual tsunami, revealing the personality and characteristics of God. Reveal the power that resurrects, renews, revives, delivers, transforms, and overcomes. Surround me with the power of your presence that belongs to me through the sacrifice of Christ Jesus. Transfer your presence to me through your Living Word, in the name of Jesus.

Thank you that even when you ascended to heaven, you left your Holy Spirit to be with me. Thank you for your glory that is available to me always. Thank you for your Shekinah Glory that is indwelling in me. I decree and declare that I make you my refuge, that I may tell all of your good works. I decree that I will put God first above all things. I decree that I dwell under the shadow of the Almighty, making Him my dwelling place. I decree that I will be a good steward over my love relationship with the Lord and the Holy Spirit.

I seal this declaration in the blood of the Lamb, and I pray all of this in the matchless name of Jesus. Amen.

SPIRITUAL ADVANCEMENT

"For promotion cometh neither from the east, nor from the west, nor from the south. But God is the judge: he putteth down one, and setteth up another."
(Psalm 75:6-7 KJV)

EL CHUWL *(ISAIAH 43:1-3)*

I lift up the Living God who elevates His people. You are the Bread of Life and the Living Waters; my soul would be dry and cracked without you. You are the God who breathes life into dead things; my inner being would be empty if it were not for your spirit. You formed me for your purpose, so that I may worship you and bring you glory. You are the potter; I am the clay. Your hands formed me to be used as an instrument of your choosing. You granted me life through your steadfast love, so that I may have life, and life more abundantly. You are the God of divine advancement; one who advances His people into greatness.

Lord, I repent for not believing that anything significant can happen through me. Forgive me if I have ever doubted the calling that you have placed on my life. Forgive me for having a poverty mindset from the lack of knowledge of your grace. I renounce every curse I may have spoken over my life to delay my advancement. I repent for my lack of belief in your ability to advance me in your kingdom.

Father, I commit myself to you to establish my plans.

"For promotion cometh neither from the east, nor from the west, nor from the south. But God is the judge: he putteth down one, and setteth up another." **(Psalm 75:6-7 KJV)**

I come to your throne, humbly asking that you ordain my steps to walk right into my promotion. Mature me in wisdom, and empower me to conform to your standards of righteousness. Through your Holy Spirit, give me more knowledge and understanding of my Lord and Savior Jesus Christ, so that I may operate in alignment with His passions. Anoint me to preach the gospel throughout the world to those who have never heard of the name of Jesus Christ, and let my outreach touch lives and lead them to the salvation of Jesus. Advance me to do your good works, so that I may hear your favorable statement, *"Well done, thou good and faithful servant."* **(Matthew 25:21b KJV)**

In the name of Jesus, progress me to move higher and higher, from faith to faith and glory to glory. Prepare me for the responsibilities of the high office that you have ordained for me in heaven. Help me commit to being a mature Christian, without being double-minded or lukewarm. Enable me to demonstrate a positive attitude toward correction, and give me a contrite, teachable, and humble spirit. You are the vine, and I am the branch; as I remain in you and you in me, fill me with the fruits of your spirit according to **Galatians 5:22**. Help me prioritize holiness, honesty, and integrity above all other virtues.

*"It is written that man shall not live by bread alone but by every word of God." (**Matthew 4:4 NIV** paraphrased)*

Holy Spirit, I call on you to empower me to be a *doer* of your Word and not just a hearer. Make me as memorable as your servant Mordecai, who was promoted from a low status to a leader. Enable me with the tenacity to stay consistent with your Word, so that I may gain the knowledge and wisdom needed to live a holy and successful life here on earth.

In the name of Jesus Christ of Nazareth, by the power of the blood, I break every yoke of distraction and stagnation against my advancement. I take up my weapon, the two-edged sword of the spirit, and I cut down the powers of witches and warlocks fighting against my advancement, in the name of Jesus. I revoke every satanic decree issued against my advancement in Jesus' mighty name. I remove my name from the book of poverty, and I destroy every plan, plot, and scheme of the enemy that tries to bring suffering into my life through lack and insufficiency. I reject every spirit of stagnation; and I annihilate every spirit hindering my advancement, in the name of Jesus. I speak against every plan to demote me or abort my calling, in the name of Jesus.

Holy Spirit, overflow my cup with the anointing to stand upright with you, and empower me to remain undefeatable in warfare. Equip me with the necessary skills to access my advancement. Lord, I thank you for the times where I have felt weak and limited, for those were the moments that brought you glory. Thank you for my spiritual growth, advancement, and elevation to do your good works. Thank you for daily ordaining my path to be filled with light. Thank you for being a father who doesn't watch me suffer but opens a realm of success for me to walk into. Thank you for advancing me today, and thank you for the fresh fire and the anointing oil of elevation.

I decree and declare that my steps are ordained by the Lord. I decree and declare that I am advancing further into the kingdom of God like never before. I decree and declare that He who began a good work in me will carry it out unto completion. I decree and declare that I am un*stoppable*, un*killable*, and un*touchable*, in the name of Jesus.

I seal this declaration in the blood of the Lamb, and I pray all of this in the matchless name of Jesus. Amen.

ACCURACY IN THE SPIRIT

"Honest scales and balances belong to the LORD; all the weights in the bag are of his making. Kings detest wrongdoing, for a throne is established through righteousness. Kings take pleasure in honest lips; they value the one who speaks what is right. A king's wrath is a messenger of death, but the wise will appease it. When a king's face brightens, it means life; his favor is like a rain cloud in spring."
(Proverbs 16:11-15 NIV)

EL EMETH *(PSALM 31:6)*

Lord, you are the God who never changes; you are the same yesterday, today, and forever. You lead us and guide us into all truth. I praise you because you never lie nor have to repent. I worship you for your unmerited grace that never runs dry. I uplift your holy name, and give you all the glory for being honest, accurate, exceptional, and just. I bless your name for being my helper…for I would be lost without your guidance.

You have searched for the one who will stand in the gap, and I come boldly to your throne saying, *"Here I am. Send me."* Holy Spirit, I yield myself to you in intercession and give you complete access to work through me. Increase my hunger to wake up in the brisk of the day to seek your face. Humble me to spend more time in your presence, so that I may be familiar with the rhythm of your heartbeat. Quiet my spirit, so I may accurately hear your voice as you reveal your secrets to me. Give me the discipline to obey you without delay when you give direction.

Holy Spirit, assist me in intercession as I pray in perfect alignment with your will and your purpose. Anoint me to be your intercessor, your watchman, your gatekeeper. Advance my prayer life in warfare as I guard the gates and keep watch. Fill my mouth with lightning as I speak the commands to strike the mark. A throne is established through righteousness. Keep me on the highway of the upright to avoid all evil, for it's the effectual fervent prayers of the righteous that availeth much.

I acknowledge that it is the way of the Lord to be fervent in spirit when speaking and teaching the things concerning Jesus. Let only the truth come off my lips when spreading the gospel and sharing my testimonies. You have promised wisdom to all those who ask, and I come to you for the gift of divine wisdom, insight, hindsight, and foresight. How much better to get wisdom than gold, insight rather than silver. Let the truth of God come off my tongue as I speak words of wisdom and give instruction. Impart in me the fear of the Lord so I will not judge by the sight of my eyes or the hearing of my ears. Guide me to discern everything with your perfect counsel. As I come into agreement with your will by faith, give me the mind of Christ to operate in Christ-centered kingdom thoughts. During times I'm called to operate prophetically, keep me completely submitted under the Holy Spirit to prophesy with complete accuracy. I pray you will take pleasure in my honest lips and be pleased with me when I speak what is right.

Father, I repent for any doors that I have opened for the enemy to chain me to the lying strongman. Forgive me for my lack of faith and knowledge of you; and help me to break the yoke of bondage and remain in you, so that I will never be yoked to the enemy again. Convict me if I lean on my own understanding and operate in my flesh.

In the name of Jesus according to **Matthew 18:18**, I bind up the lying spirit that breeds the fruits of deception, flattery, religious bondage, superstition, false prophecy, lies, accusations, gossip, slander, and false teaching. Whatsoever I bind on earth shall be bound in heaven, and whatsoever I lose on earth will be loosed in heaven. In the name of Jesus, I loosen the spirit of truth over my life. Shine your face upon me, and loosen a new life as your favor rains over me like a cloud in spring.

Thank you for imparting in me the ability to pray and intercede with accuracy, effectiveness, and Dunamis power. Thank you for giving me the skills like David, so that every time I pick up my sword, I do not miss my target. I thank you for the Holy Spirit that lives in me, teaching me all things and empowering me to do all things.

I decree and declare that I will heed to the instructions of the Lord. I decree and declare that I will trust in the Lord and lean not on my own understanding but acknowledge you in every way. I decree and declare that I will be wise and discerning and give gracious words to promote instruction. I decree and declare that I will be fully submitted and led by the Holy Spirit in giving prophetic words. I decree and declare that I will pray in spirit and truth at all times. I decree and declare that I will not give attention to any strange voices around me, but that I will always follow my Great

Shepherd. I decree and declare that I am led by wisdom, using divine insight and foresight to remain accurate in the spirit, in the name of Jesus.

I seal this declaration in the blood of the Lamb, and I pray all of this in the matchless name of Jesus. Amen.

SPIRITUAL WARFARE

SPIRITUAL WARFARE TESTIMONY

I was born into a family that is very familiar with the kingdom of darkness through the practice of witchcraft and black magic. I always knew I was a different kind of person, but I didn't know what it was about me. I was never really able to fit in the way I wanted to. I was always with the cool kids, but I never really felt like I belonged. I would experience things as a child that I couldn't speak to anyone about because I knew they would think I was crazy, so I kept everything to myself. I had no idea that this whole time, I've been sensitive to the spiritual world. It wasn't until about four years ago, when I was twenty-three years old, that I realized that I am not crazy, and that I have been living in two different worlds.

My first spiritual experience happened when I was living in Pomona, California with my paternal grandmother, Cynthia. I was six or seven years old at the time and let me tell you…I was living lavish. Grandma Cynthia owned a beautiful two-storey home next to a golf course. It had an amazing view, and it was surrounded by palm trees. I can still smell the fresh air and feel the warmth of that California sun. Aside from living the good life, Grandma Cynthia was a strong woman of God. She was kind, giving, compassionate, respected, and loved by many. Her love for people was a manifestation of her acceptance of Jesus Christ as her personal Savior, and her abiding faith in Christ was felt by all who knew her. She worked at Kaiser Permanente as the Director of Volunteer Services, where she touched the lives of many patients and their families. She was a woman of God who was very wise and knew how to apply the Scripture that said, *"Train up a child in the way he should go and when he is old, he will not depart from it."* **(Proverbs 22:6 NIV)**

Grandma Cynthia kept me in church. I went to children's church where we fellowshipped and had Bible study. For me, church was boring until it was time for me to perform. I would perform skits in front of the congregation, and that's where I really came alive. I was living as a normal Christian child—and then one day, I woke up, and things were never the same.

One night, after falling into a deep sleep, I had a dream. I was walking up a black spiral staircase. There were many flights of stairs; and when you looked down, it was a long way to the bottom. The next thing I knew, I was free falling down the middle. I remember the feeling of falling in the dream; it felt so real that I thought I was falling to my death. I woke up in a panic, breathing heavily. I had never experienced anything like that before; a dream that felt so real. I can remember it so clearly because it tormented me for a long time. This was the first of many dreams that felt completely real, where I was conscious enough to feel every emotion, and sometimes, even excruciating pain.

Grandma Cynthia passed away six months after I moved in with her, and this nearly broke me to pieces. I'm grateful that God allowed me to spend that time with her before she passed because otherwise, I probably would never have met her. After her passing, my father came and picked me up, and I moved back to my great-grandmother Ruth's house in Brooklyn.

My father had a best friend named Andy who was his right-hand man. Andy was my godfather, and he always looked out for me. I was very close to his daughter—we were like sisters. One summer, Andy was riding his motorcycle when he crashed and was killed instantly. Shortly after this happened, I started waking up in the middle of the night and seeing Andy standing by my bed. I slept in my Grandma Ruth's bed every night, and one night, I opened my eyes to see Andy lying next to me. I could have been hallucinating, but this completely freaked me out as a kid. I thought I was going insane.

At this point, I was convinced I could see dead people; and if that wasn't enough, when I was about fifteen years old, I started having lucid dreams again. (Lucid dreaming is when you are aware that you are dreaming, and you have the ability to control your dreams, the outcomes, or even the environment around you while you're still dreaming.) This time, it was turned up a notch. One night, I was sleeping and had a dream that I was walking across the street by my house, and somebody shot me. I couldn't see their face, but I could literally feel the bullet going through me. As it went through my body, I felt the intense pain of having just been shot.

I've had this dream of being shot numerous times. If I wasn't dreaming about being shot, I was dreaming about my teeth being pulled out of my mouth…and if I could only explain to you the excruciating pain I felt in the middle of that dream. I would feel the pain in my dream; and I wanted it to stop so badly, but I couldn't wake myself out of the nightmare.

I hated it. I started researching and trying to understand what exactly my dreams meant, but I could never find a clear explanation. I was lucid dreaming.

Strangely enough, after having the dream about my teeth being pulled out and being in excruciating pain, my great-grandmother Ruth passed away, and that's exactly what I felt…but this time, the pain was in the natural. I don't know if I had a peculiar imagination or I could really see dead people, because soon after my grandmother passed, I started seeing her in the house. I was battling all of these supernatural experiences with no one to talk to. I had so many other lucid dreams, and I didn't understand what was happening to me.

As I got older, the dreams decreased for some time, possibly because I was too high off of weed or drunk off of a bottle to remember or feel anything. I thought I was just living my life—until things took a turn in a whole different direction. It was the day I became spiritually "woke," and I never saw the world the same way again.

This testimony is similar to the one I spoke of in my Spiritual Advancement Testimony; except here, I will go more into depth. It all started when I was in the entertainment industry. I was pursuing a career as a tattoo model, celebrity host, actress, video vixen, and brand ambassador. I appeared on VH1 Black Ink Crew and The Maury Show on NBC. What I thought was a rising career turned into a valley of destruction.

I had just gotten signed to a management label where I met "Josh" (pseudonym), and he introduced me to the video *The Secret Laws of Attraction*, a life hack on how to manifest anything you desire through the power of your mind. People use it to manifest love and relationships, money and wealth, improve their mental and physical health, attract success and abundance through affirmations, frequencies, visions, meditation, and training their subconscious mind. Some even go as far as the activation of their "third eye," thought to be found in the pineal gland, which is an eye gate located in the middle of the forehead that helps one tap into the realms of the spirit for a higher consciousness. The third eye is also associated with wisdom and a keen intuition. For people into chakras, it is known as the highest chakra in your body.

Although this may seem great, there are many dangers attached to it. It's a dangerous delusion that makes you believe that you are in fact your own god, and there's no room to acknowledge Christ for anything in your life because the belief is *"I have absolute control over my life and my destiny."* Quoting affirmations such as, *"I love money, and money loves me."* There are also dangers in activating the third eye, including lucid dreams and nightmares, intuitions, believing you are invincible or superhuman, astral projection, developing a sensitivity to light, sun, and vivid colors, and chaotic behavior.

> *"There will be terrible times in the last days. People will be lovers of themselves, lovers of money, boastful, proud, abusive, disobedient to their parents, ungrateful, unholy, without love, unforgiving, slanderous, without self-control, brutal, not lovers of the good, treacherous, rash, conceited, lovers of pleasure rather than lovers of God, having a form of godliness but denying its power. Have nothing to do with such people."* **(2 Timothy 3:1-5 NIV)**

2 Timothy 3:1-5 is a perfect description of the world we are living in today, where New Age spirituality is taking over. For the Christians who meditate and quote affirmations, don't hear me wrong. I love affirmations, and I meditate…but I meditate on the Word of God, and I affirm the myself through the Word of God, leaving room to acknowledge Christ and give Him the glory when I see the manifestation of what He did for me. *That's* the difference.

Before I received this revelation, I watched *The Secret Laws of Attraction* twice, and I was instantly intrigued. After watching it, I watched many other spiritual videos, and that led me on a journey "down the rabbit hole." As I went through "the matrix," I couldn't see the world, people, or even nature the same. I couldn't watch TV shows or movies without pointing out all of the subliminal messages and symbols that confirmed how corrupt the government was. Government conspiracies became my new obsession.

I was watching government conspiracy videos, reading books, and doing research day and night. When I got hooked on these videos, I became convinced that my whole entire life had been a lie, and it was time that I unlearned everything I once knew and relearned the "truth" that the government had been hiding from me. I spent the majority of my time on the web and on YouTube, studying and researching "the truth." When I had to go outside, I would feel like I was melting. I couldn't go anywhere or do anything because I hated being around people. I would look at them with disgust, because I thought everybody was "asleep" because they were not enlightened like I was, not realizing that I was really the one who was "asleep "on the inside. I couldn't go outside, especially in the daylight, because the light made my skin crawl, and I would instantly go into a fit of rage. I was only able to function during the witching hours.

If I wasn't watching videos about government conspiracies, I was watching videos about New Age spirituality. I learned how to activate my third eye and the art of manifesting, I studied twin flames, how to speak to the universe, numerology, elevating vibrations (chakras), sage, crystals, divination, and more. I thought that I reached a new level in my spiritual walk because I started seeing the "Angel Numbers:" 11:11, 111, 222, 333, 444, and so on.

> *Angel numbers are associated with numerology, the language of the universe that represents a hidden language of energy, frequency, and vibration. Also known as "guardian angels," sending us signs through repeating numbers.*

I would see these consecutive numbers repeating no matter where I was or what I was doing; and I believed that the universe was speaking to me, and that I was talking back to it. I knew then that I had the power to control the universe…and I was in fact God.

I believed I was my own god, and that I had the power to control everything that happened around me. I worshiped the universe—the moon, and the stars—and I changed my entertainment name to Blu Indigo to represent the colors of the universe. I would go to the Botanicas (a store where New Age paraphernalia is sold) to get my weekly tarot card reading and restock my spiritual baths and oils. I started investing in crystals and wearing them around my neck, learning how to "recharge my energy" through them. I would buy Hamsa necklaces and evil eye bracelets and put them on my son for protection.

The Hamsa is a palm-shaped amulet used as a sign of protection against the evil eye that is believed to deliver bad luck and negative energy. The Hamsa is also believed to bring good luck, fertility, and abundance.

I was committed to this lifestyle. I started practicing yoga because I believed that it was a good way to clear my mind and align my thoughts with the universe. I thought that this was a great idea because my mind was always racing. Through meditation, I learned to hypnotize myself. I will not share the process but take my word for it that self-hypnosis is in fact real. My mind was clear and empty, alright…empty enough for every demon and devil in hell to enter into my mind and have its way.

Not too long after activating my third eye and beginning my involvement with the occult, I started hearing strange voices telling me to commit suicide. When I would get upset enough, I would cut my wrists until I bled, and I tried to overdose on pills. I've heard these voices tell me to jump in front of moving cars or trains. The voices were telling me to kill my child as I received many visions of him dying and followed behind it was my desire to do so. I began to experience a high level of paranormal activity in my home, hearing things moving or seeing dark shadows. I had never felt so lost, broken, dark, and demonic in my life. Satan had such a grip on me at this time that I completely gave in. I started researching how I could sell my soul to the devil. I reached out to some people that I knew had made agreements with Satan, and I completely stopped caring about the particulars. If it was a blood sacrifice Satan needed, I had a list of family members that I didn't mind seeing in a casket. I even started writing the mark of the beast (triple six) on my papers…and when I was twenty-five years old, I accepted Satan into my life.

BUT GOD…

You know how this story ends. I was saved and delivered from every demon and devil that I allowed into my life. I am also an attempted suicide survivor. Although I cut my wrists and popped pills with the intention to overdose, it didn't kill me. It was nothing but the blood of Jesus that prevailed over the spirit of death. As I mentioned before, my grandmother was a woman of God who knew that when you raise a child up in the way they should go, they will not depart from it. No matter how far I strayed, I was still close enough to God to return back to Him, and He delivered me and broke the curse of the occult and New Age spirituality off my life, along with many other generational curses.

I stand today in liberty. I no longer practice or participate in anything involving New Age spirituality. I am now the Generational Curse Breaker in my bloodline because of it. Had I not accepted the Lord's invitation when I did, I don't know if I would have even been alive to tell you this story. As a matter a fact, I know I would not; because when I chose to worship Satan, I chose death.

BUT THEN HERE CAME SATAN...

Just when I thought it was over, I found out that Satan was not ready to let me go without a fight. Four months after being saved and delivered, I was on fire for God, and this handsome man caught my attention. In December of 2019, I realized that I had fallen in love with him. If you're thinking that there is nothing wrong with that... I'll be glad to tell you why it's wrong. Everything is wrong with that scenario in the eyes of the Lord because *I was legally married*. Although we were separated and living in separate homes, this was still a sin of adultery, and God was not pleased.

It started with a harmless text here and there; and then we progressed to Facetime calls, making each other laugh, as we spent hours on the phone, trying to learn more and more about each other every day. I'm a tough cookie to crumble when it comes to falling in love; but with him, I couldn't help but give him all of my time and attention. He became the apple of my eye. I guess every cookie gets soft when dipped in milk, and I was convinced he came straight from the land flowing with milk and honey. I was in awe. I have been in a lot of relationships before, but I had never met a man like him. This was my first encounter with a man who was sweet, caring, kind, giving, a loving Christian man, and someone who accepted me for who I was and never judged me for my past. I could talk to him about anything, and he loved my son like his own. As much as I tried, I couldn't resist him. What I really mean is that I *could* have... but I really didn't *want* to.

Falling in love was new to me. No matter who I was with, I never surrendered my heart to anyone like I did to him…not even to my own husband. With him, I felt that I had someone who truly meant the world to me. Little did I know Satan was in the background plotting his next move; and unfortunately, I fell into his trap. I realized that I was caught up in the sin of idolatry. Whatever you give the majority of your time and attention to becomes an idol, because it is what you subconsciously worship. I was giving him more time and attention than I was giving God, and that caused me to reject God yet again.

We thought being on the phone was harmless—but the problem came when we stayed on the phone twenty-four/seven. We had a serious problem hanging up the phone. We were talking on the phone during the witching hours (midnight to three in the morning), and you know no good can come out of that because that's when the witches and warlocks come out to play. Due to our lack of self-control, what started out as a harmless crush transformed into an ungodly soul tie. This became a major issue not only in my life but also in my ministry.

> *A soul tie is when two souls become joined together as one. There are **godly** soul ties and **ungodly** soul ties. **Godly** soul ties are soul ties you may have with your parents or children which have positive impact on your life. **Ungodly** soul ties happen when you are joined to someone outside of marriage through sex or other forms of communication that have a negative impact on your life.*

I knew that I was still married, but I didn't want to let go of the love, time, attention, and commitment that he gave me. I was aware that Satan had his hand all up in this because my mind, my priorities, and my desires were all screwed up. Trust me…God was NOT pleased with my decisions. The conviction was ripping me to shreds, and grieving the Holy Spirit weighed on me terribly. He was also a man of God who was filled with the Holy Spirit, and we agreed it was time we needed to follow our convictions and get right with God.

What we were involved in was an ungodly soul tie, and we tried our best to break it off, but it felt almost impossible. In our efforts to break the soul tie, we would try to stay away from each other, but we couldn't last twenty-four hours without finding our way right back. We would be fine for one day; but by the next, we felt like somebody we loved had just died. We were both having episode after episode of emotional breakdowns. I was in love with this man, and the thought of losing him crushed my heart. I knew in order to break the soul tie, we had to stop everything we were doing, meaning no more talking on the phone, texting, or hanging out, until we completely starved every ungodly thought or desire.

Believe me when I say this was no easy task. I wrestled with it, and I could not comprehend the thought of not being with him. I would spend days crying my heart out and came up with a thousand excuses not to let him go. I felt pulled between him and God, asking myself who I wanted more. He was my best friend. We were so in sync that we would see each other and happen to have on matching outfits unknowingly. We talked the same, prayed the same, knew each other's darkest secrets, and knew what the other was thinking at that very moment. The thought of being with someone else disturbed me, and the thought of him being with someone else would send me into a rage.

The hardest part of all of this was that we go to the same church. Imagine trying to separate yourself from someone you have to see three times a week… can you say, "messy ministry?" If seeing each other wasn't bad enough, you have no idea what it's like to be laid out on the altar, going through multiple deliverances; screaming, crying, travailing, and repenting because you decided to have sex the night before. Or what about when you are lifting your hands in worship, trying to give it all to the Lord, but then the enemy reminds you of the night before, when you were intimate with one another, and you find yourself worshiping your orgasms.

I couldn't even focus on the sermon because the way he bit his lips turned me on. God forbid a woman come near him. I was ready to declare war because I was *not* having it. I was so caught up in the weight of my sin that the fruit began to show. I began to isolate myself from the congregation, and I threw fits of frustration toward anyone who tried to help. This right here is the mighty effect of an ungodly soul tie and idolatry.

I urge you to understand that STDs are real! I'm not talking about sexually transmitted diseases…I'm talking about Sexually Transmitted *Demons*. They create this demonic soul tie that links you spiritually with the person that you slept with. These are toxic soul ties (also known as twin flames) that make you feel like you cannot live without someone. You feel spiritually and emotionally attached to them; and no matter what they do, you cannot separate yourself from them. You think about them all day long, having flashbacks to the times you were intimate, and you feel as if you can feel them even if they're not with you. You share each other's emotions; when they are sad, you are sad; when they are happy, you are happy; when they are angry, you are angry. It is almost like you have lost your identity, and you have become one flesh. You take on their negative traits and begin to act like them and talk like them. You defend your relationship and refuse to accept advice from anyone. You become controlling, abusive, and maybe even stalkerish. You stay with them, even if they treat you terribly and are bad for you.

These are some signs you may have an ungodly soul tie on your hands. These kinds of relationships can end up deadly, not just physically but spiritually. I was one who had soul ties; and not only did I take on their demons, but I took on the demons of every person they been with as well. These are what I call Sexually Transmitted Demons.

I admit that I struggled to stay out of the sheets, not because I was addicted to having sex (because I wasn't) but because in my mind, I had this idea that if I didn't do it, someone else would. Or because of the jealousy issues that I had, I had to make sure I solidified my spot in his life by keeping his mind on me at all times. At the same time, I didn't have enough revelation in me to stay out of his bed. I knew that it was wrong, and I wanted to end it…but knowing that it was wrong wasn't enough to make me stop. Let me tell you. Our God is a jealous God, and *He was not having it.* Can I be transparent with you? I became really reckless, and it came back to bite me in the behind later.

My church is a very prophetic church, and we often have guests come and release prophetic words if the Lord gives them the unction. This was never a fun time for me because every time someone came to give a word, they seemed to call him out and say to him, *"You have got a flirtatious spirit around you. Don't get distracted."* Not only was this embarrassing to me because the majority of the people who know about us knew how much I loved him, but it was also heartbreaking. I felt as if I was taking him away from Christ and being a distraction in his life. The first two times I heard the word go forth, I tried to pay it no mind and keep doing what I wanted to do, but the third time was the final straw for me.

At that moment, I was done with God, and I was done with church. I was so mad at God. I asked him, *"Why did you let me get my heart broken like that? Why did you let me be humiliated?"* I wanted God to cover me and not expose my sin, but it didn't happen the way I wanted it to. I was ready to run out of the church and never return, but my pastor did not let me walk away. She didn't let me forsake my position or give up on God. She told me that I am a warrior and reminded me of God's promises, then told me to get back out there and worship through it. I will never forget how broken and embarrassed I felt, because God was stripping me of everything I knew and loved, and it hurt worse than the six hours of labor I went through with my son. I remember standing at the altar, holding on to the Scripture, *"Though he slay me, yet will I trust him"* **(Job 13:15 KJV)**. As I was meditating on this Scripture, I was worshiping with tears in my eyes and praying through the pain with a broken spirit.

When I went home that night, every part of me wanted to give up and throw in the towel, but God wouldn't let me. He gave me enough strength to keep pressing. I found that my moments of brokenness were when I prayed the most effectively, because God used my weakness to show His strength through me, so that people were able to see that it wasn't me praying it through, it was God praying through me.

I said many times "the thought" of letting him go or "the thought" of losing him. That stronghold in my mind kept me in a place where I couldn't move past that "thought." It took some time; but after finally making up our minds, we decided that we were going to let go, completely turn away from sin, and live a consecrated life. We made up our minds to trust God and give the situation to Him, so that if He chooses to resurrect the relationship, it will be His will and not ours. Now that it's all said and done, I think we both agree that God knew what was best for us. We would have destroyed one another because we were not ready to take on each other's issues when God had so much work that He still needed to do in us.

I still needed to be healed from my past—the rejection that I faced, the anger and jealousy, the mommy and daddy issues—and I needed to get to know who I was and who I am in Christ. Plus, whatever God does, He wants to get the glory from; and in this particular situation, there was no room for His glory to shine through. As hard as it was to let go, we continue to hold on to His promise and remember that whatever is in the perfect will of the Father He will always bless, because His plans are to prosper us and not to harm us *(Jeremiah 29:11)*.

I am so grateful that we serve a God who is full of mercy and grace, because sin will leave us feeling condemned. I thought I was going straight to hell after everything I did, but there is no condemnation in Christ because His love endures forever. I know I am forgiven, and I have even forgiven myself. And since I have changed the sheets and closed the door, I can focus on the Cross. Although it hurt, I am grateful that God did it the way He did, because He knew exactly what I needed and how I needed it to provoke the change.

> *The weight of sin is a heavy one...but I would rather carry the weight of His glory than the weight of my sin. Freedom feels so much better.*

I learned from this experience that not only is healing extremely important before getting into a relationship, but I first have to know how to be a wife to my bridegroom (Jesus). If I don't know how to be a good wife to Christ, I can never be a good wife to any man. After separating from the soul tie, there were so many toxic relationship habits that God began to reveal to me. I had to be set free and healed from them before I could even look at a man. Whew! I thank God for that because I would have gone straight into another relationship, and it would have been over before it even began. I would have been carrying all that toxic waste with me, then infecting him with it. This is proof alone that we should trust God because He knows what's best for us.

Satan's job is to kill, steal, and destroy. I was at war from the time I was born because my mother's side of the family is very familiar with the kingdom of darkness. I was born into a family that practiced witchcraft and black magic. This led to many events that I had no control over and some that I had a choice over. The enemy was plotting to take me out when he knew the assignment God had placed on my life. He came for my soul many times; and if he couldn't have my soul, then he tried to trip me up in my walk with Christ. I learned throughout my mistakes not to give the enemy any room. Not a *cracked door*...not an *inch*...not a *second*...not the *time. of. day.*

As I remain in God and keep my mind on Him, I know I am safe. As I remain in His Word and in prayer, it is much easier to resist temptation. I am far from perfect, and I know there is much more that God has to do in and through me; but I have peace knowing as long as I am putting Him first, walking upright, praying consistently, worshiping Him, and reading His Word, I will see the goodness of the Lord. Living like this, you can never go wrong...it's like you become spiritually bulletproof. It was far from easy, but I sacrificed my flesh and my Isaac, and now I can testify that what the enemy meant for evil, God has worked out for my good.

If you are like me and have ungodly soul ties, there are ways you can break them. When you accept Christ as your Lord and Savior, He will begin to do a great work in you. Not only will He deliver you from your demons and break curses, but He will also assist you in breaking ungodly soul ties, so that you can put Him first.

> *"Be strong in the Lord, and put on the whole armor of God, that ye may be able to stand against the wiles of the devil."*
> ***(Ephesians 6:11 KJV)***

REVERSE THE CURSE

"It is for freedom that Christ has set us free. Stand firm, then, and do not let yourselves be burdened again by a yoke of slavery."
(Galatians 5:1 NIV)

JEHOVAH NISSI (DEUTERONOMY 20:3-4)

I bless the Lord my God who is great, mighty, and awesome in power. You are the Way, the Truth, and the Life. You have the power to break and to build; to uproot and to plant. Praise the Lord, for you are the yoke destroyer and the burden bearer.

In the mighty name of Jesus Christ and by the power of the blood of Jesus Christ, I confess that I am serving a Holy God and His name is Jesus.

I put on the whole armor of God; the breastplate of righteousness, the shield of faith, the helmet of salvation, the belt of truth, the shoes of the gospel of peace, and the sword of the spirit, which is the Word of God. I boldly declare that I am dead to the evil works of the enemy. I rebuke the devil and all his negative influence in my life. I break the chain of bad habits that causes the same cycle of sin. I receive permanent deliverance from every bad habit. I curse the witchcraft, spells, black magic, white magic, jinxes, and enchantments that may be working against my life, in the name of Jesus.

I renounce all satanic contracts and covenants with the spirit of death. I sever every soul tie and stronghold working against me. I shut the door to every demonic spiritual portal. I arrest the spirits who operate in the use of sand, bones, sacrifices, tea leaves, tarot cards, palm readings, lumps on the head, Ouija boards, crystal balls, occult computer games, charms, crystals, and drugs, in the matchless name of Jesus.

I bind and rebuke, in the name of Jesus, the spirit of divination and all its evil works in the form of fortune telling, witches and warlocks, stargazing, rebellion, water witching, hypnosis, and enchantment. I reject satanic intelligence and seek divine wisdom from the Holy Spirit.

I speak to every familiar spirit that has attached itself to me though yoga, sages, or contacting my ancestors, and I command you to be broken off of me, in the name of Jesus.

I boldly declare that Christ has given me the authority and Dunamis power against unclean spirits. Prince of the air, hear ye therefore my voice. I am no longer subject to your authority and your influence will no longer find access to my life nor my flesh. I break every controlling power ruling over my life, in the name of Jesus.

I break every chain and destroy every yoke from the spirit of anger, greed, bitterness, hatred, malice, and jealousy that is manifesting in my life. I command you to come out of your hiding place and enter no more. I bind and cast out every lying and deceptive spirit, in the mighty name of Jesus. I overrule every spirit of bondage, alcoholism, smoking, addiction to drugs, and gambling. I command you to lose your grip on my life. I render naught every power of the air that influences me into negative actions or thoughts. I boldly declare that I am not your candidate, and I cast you out of my life. I speak destruction to every spirit of rebellion and disobedience in my life, in the name of Jesus.

I purge myself of every spirit of whoredom, filthiness, perversion, lust, adultery, fornication, sexual immortality, and bondage from the spirit of the world. I uproot every seed of Satan in my mind and tell you to dry up now by the fire of the Holy Spirit. I boldly declare that I am delivered from the company of bad friends. I wash my brain, eyes, and mind with the precious blood of Christ Jesus. I remove all bad habits and evil thoughts which are physically and spiritually engraved.

I send every satanic influence that has come into my life into the bottomless pit of hell and chain it there forever. I confess that I believe that no affliction of bad habits or negative thought patterns will come to me a second time. I fully submit myself to the guidance of the Holy Spirit.

Father, I invite you into my heart. Help me to stay on the side of righteousness and not step into Satan's territory ever again.

I affect and enforce God's words and promises. I decree that my mind is restored. I decree and declare that every spell is broken off of my life and my bloodline. I decree that every satanic influence that has been destroyed today will not reoccur again. I decree my body is the temple of the Holy Spirit for Him to dwell in. I decree and declare that I am now free from sinful habits and profitable for the Master's use, ready for my assignment. I decree and declare that Satan has no power over me. Where the spirit of the Lord dwells, there is freedom; and I decree that who the Son sets free is free indeed! I thank you for calling me out of the darkness into your marvelous light. Declaration brings possession, and I shall have what I have declared.

I seal this declaration in the blood of the Lamb, and I pray all of this in the matchless name of Jesus. Amen.

DELIVERANCE DECLARATION

"For he has rescued us from the dominion of darkness and brought us into the kingdom of the Son he loves."
(Colossians 1:13 NIV)

EL CHAIYAI (*JEREMIAH 10:10*)

Lord, you are my rock, my fortress, and my deliverer. You are my shield and my horn of salvation. I believe that you are the Son of God. I believe that you died on the Cross for my sins, you rose from the dead, and you sit at the right hand of the Father. You are my hiding place; the God who protects me from all trouble and surrounds me with songs of deliverance. I believe that I am your child, and I have the power to overcome, because greater is He who is in me than He who is in the world.

I repent, renounce, and ask your forgiveness for every sin I have committed, spoken, or thought out of rebellion, disobedience, weakness, or ignorance. I repent and renounce every curse and sinful word that I have ever spoken or thought about you, my Lord. I repent and renounce every sinful thought or curse that I have spoken against your anointed ones. I repent and renounce every act of disobedience, dishonor, evil thought, or curse that I have committed against my earthly parents and my spiritual parents, in the name of Jesus.

I break every chain and destroy every yoke off of myself and my family due to blasphemy, rebellion, or cursing you. I speak that God's anointing will destroy every curse against me or my family through our bloodline from past generations. I destroy every vow and judgment that I have placed on both my birth parents and spiritual parents. I now break all curses that were brought on me by these sins, in the name of Jesus.

I repent for all my contacts with Satan and his evil works. I renounce all involvement with witchcraft, New Age spirituality, and the occult. I repent and renounce all demonic spirits that I have given access to enter my life. I renounce all of the curses that were handed down through my family from prior generations. I do not choose to participate in or affiliate myself with any of the sins practiced by my ancestors. I confess that I forgive my parents and my ancestors for causing these curses to come upon my life. I lay down and cast away resentment, bitterness, hatred, rebellion, and disobedience. I cast down every vain imagination and every high thing that exalts itself against the knowledge of God; and with your divine power, I demolish all strongholds, in the name of Jesus.

I cry out to you and ask you to deliver me from distress. Lord God, I ask that you forgive me for sinning against you. Forgive me and cleanse me by your precious blood. I receive your forgiveness, and I forgive myself for falling short of your glory. Sin shall no longer be my master; because I am not subject under the law, but I am saved by your grace.

I put on the full armor of God, and I take my stand against the devil's schemes. The Word of God says that no weapon formed against me shall prosper, and every tongue that rises against me in judgment shall be condemned. Satan, by the power of spirit of the Lord, I am raising up a standard against you, and by the power of the blood, I declare you have no power over me, my life, my family, or my finances any longer. I leave no room for you; I now cancel every assignment you have planned against me. I revoke every legal right you claim to remain. I have served you notice; you must pack your bags and leave me now, touching or harming no one else, in the name of Jesus.

Lord, you said if I call upon your name I will be delivered, and I call upon your matchless name and confess you as my deliverer. Thank you for lifting the burden off my shoulders and breaking the yoke from my neck, destroying it because of the fresh anointing on my life.

Thank you for setting me free, so that I may stand firm, no longer burdened by a yoke of slavery. Thank you, Christ Jesus, for the law of the Spirit who gives life, and for setting me free from the law of sin and death. Thank you for giving me the authority to trample upon the lion and the cobra. Thank you for showing me the salvation of the Lord that was accomplished through this prayer today. Thank you for being a victorious warrior, restoring my salvation, and filling me with shouts of joy. Thank you for fighting against my enemies and giving me the victory.

I decree that I am loosed from every demon spirit working against me. I decree that I am loosed from the hands of the enemy, and I abide under the shadow of the Almighty. I decree and declare that I am strong in the Lord and in the power of His might. I declare I will not let myself be burdened again by the yoke of slavery.

I decree and declare that I have received my deliverance certificate.

I seal this declaration in the blood of the Lamb, and I pray all of this, in the matchless name of Jesus. Amen.

SOUL TIE SEVER

"It is God's will that you should be sanctified: that you should avoid sexual immorality; that each of you should learn to control your own body in a way that is holy and honorable, not in passionate lust like the pagans, who do not know God."
(1 Thessalonians 4:3-5 NIV)

ELOHIM KEDOSHIM (JOSHUA 24:19)

I give you all the glory and all the praise for your faithfulness, love, and unending mercies upon my life. I approach your throne of grace, asking for your forgiveness for engaging in the acts of sexual immorality that have opened the doors to ungodly soul ties, commitments, contracts, vows, lust, adultery, sexual misconduct, fornication, and idolatry.

Lord, I know that you are full of mercy and grace. I have confessed my sins, and I believe that you are faithful and just to forgive me of my sins and purify me from all unrighteousness. Release all unforgiveness and bitterness in my heart. I receive your forgiveness, and I forgive myself for participating in ungodly activities. May God Himself, the pure and holy God, sanctify me through and through.

Purify my heart, and renew a right spirit within me. Fill me with your love, and heal the broken areas in my heart, so that rejection and loneliness will not provoke me into sexual sin, in the name of Jesus.

Lord, I call on you to sever all ungodly soul ties between myself and anyone else. Break every soul tie formed by unnatural, ungodly relationships, sexual relations, vows, commitments, and contracts that I have made, whether knowingly or unknowingly. I renounce and release myself from all vows and contracts, and I rebuke any future attempts, in the name of Jesus.

Your Word is sharper than any double-edged sword, penetrating even to dividing soul and spirit, joints and marrow; it judges the thoughts and attitudes of the heart. Let your Word come alive right now, and effectively cut through and sever these soul ties. Grant me the discernment to know what is of God and what is not of God. Help me restrain myself from desire and thoughts of lust. For the weapons of our warfare are not carnal, but mighty in God for pulling down strongholds. Through your divine power, I now demolish every stronghold and cast down every vain imagination that exalts itself higher than the knowledge of God, and I hold every thought captive to the obedience of Christ Jesus. I demolish all strongholds that try to return me back to my own vomit, in the name of Jesus.

For our struggle is not against flesh and blood, but against the rulers, authorities, and powers of this dark world, and against the spiritual forces of evil in the heavenly realms. I choose to be united with the Lord…make me one with you in spirit instead. I forget the unions, and I release my soul from every ungodly soul tie. Through your spirit, I am empowered with self-control and do not give into the temptations of sexual desire, sexual immorality, fornication, and lust, in the name of Jesus.

I now have the power to stand firm against the lust of the eyes, the lust of the flesh, and the pride of life. May my whole spirit, soul, and body be kept spotless and without blemish at the coming of our Lord Jesus Christ. I now present my body back to you, holy and cleansed.

I seal this declaration in the blood of the Lamb, and I pray all of this in the matchless name of Jesus. Amen.

VICTORY OVER FEAR

"For God hath not given us the spirit of fear; but of power,
and of love, and of a sound mind"
(2 Timothy 1:7 KJV)

EL HAGADOL *(DEUTERONOMY 10:17)*

You are a mighty God, fearless and strong in battle. When I am afraid, I put my trust in you. I receive gratefully the comfort of the Holy Spirit. I put my trust in Him who goes *with* me and *before* me. If the Lord is with me, who shall be against me? What can mere mortals do to me? The Lord is my light and my salvation. Whom shall I fear?

On this day, I choose to confront all my fears and worries. Even though I walk through the valley of the shadow of death, I boldly declare that I will fear no evil, for my God is with me.

Lord, you are my protector. I will not fear the terror of the night, nor the arrow that flies by day; nor the pestilence that stalks in the darkness, nor the plague that destroys at midday, because you are my shield and my rampart in whom I take refuge; my God who subdues people under me.

I repent for any worry or fear that has caused me to be spiritually paralyzed. I rise above the spirit of fear, and I command all of the enemy's fear and paralyzing schemes to return back to sender, in the name of Jesus. For the spirit of fear is not for me—rather, it is for my enemies. Though a host of demons encamp against me, my heart will not fear. I boldly declare that the Lord is my strong tower. I do not *choose* fear. I do not *make friends* with fear. I will not *entertain* fear. I will not accept or engage with any spirit of fear that tries to torment my life. Satan, your works are broken.

I resist all of the fruits produced from fear. I bind and rebuke the spirits of anxiety, depression, anger, rejection, unforgiveness, control, indulgence, and insecurity. I decree love, power, and a sound mind over my life, in the name of Jesus. I decree and declare that I am free from the fear of man, fear of the future, fear of loneliness, fear of failure, fear of rejection, fear of abandonment, fear of success, and the fear of death. I decree and declare that the Goliath of fear that tries to torment my life is dead. I decree that the spirit of fear is defeated, and I receive the anointing for battle, in the name of Jesus.

Father, make me perfect in love, for it is written that there is no fear in love, because perfect love drives out fear. Fill me with perfect love that will overflow in and through me. Give me the words of wisdom that none of my adversaries will be able to resist or contradict. I draw near to you with a sincere heart full of assurance.

I decree that I will win in life, and that the spirit of fear will not keep me from reaching my destiny. Fear will not keep me from what God has promised me. Fear will not keep me from reaching the Promised Land…the land flowing with milk and honey. Activate the plans you have to prosper me and your plans for hope and a future. I enter into the most holy place by the blood of Jesus.

Father, you say to be anxious about nothing but pray about

everything, I present my request to you, asking that you guard my heart and my mind. By the power of your spirit, I declare that I will face every challenge boldly and courageously. I now walk in victory with your power that is within me. The only fear for me is the godly fear for thee.

I seal this declaration in the blood of the Lamb, and I pray all of this in the matchless name of Jesus. Amen.

PROTECTION

PROTECTION TESTIMONY

There are so many stories in the Bible about how God protected His children. There's the famous story of how He used Moses to split the Red Sea and bring a nation out of slavery *(Exodus 14:21)*. Another great story is when God protected Paul in the middle of a shipwreck *(Acts 27:27-28:5)*. The story about Daniel in the lion's den *(Daniel 6)*, Jonah when he was swallowed by a whale *(Jonah 1)*, and the adulterous woman who was about to be stoned to death *(John 8:1-11)*. There's the story of Rahab in the Book of *Joshua*, and one of my personal favorites, the story of Esther *(Esther 8-10)*, when God protected her and her people from being killed.

We have all of these stories about God's divine protection; and yet, there are people who still live their lives in fear. There are still people who blame God for unfortunate things like the death of a family member or a loved one. We get sick and feel like God has forsaken us. We look at what's going on in the world and blame God for letting it all happen. Sometimes, we may forget what God has done in our lives or allow the pride inside of us to cause us to think that we are untouchable. Other times, we just simply don't know

God or understand Him, so it's much easier to judge Him.

I come to bring you good news...

God never changes! He is the same yesterday, today, and forever *(Hebrews 13:8)*. The way He protected His children during biblical times is the same way He protects them now. Listen. I get it. Some of you may have read or heard of these stories in the Bible, but you still don't believe. Some of you may have never read or even heard of these stories, and you are just dead set on how you feel. So, I give my testimony as proof that God still is a defender and a protector.

With everything that we have been through and with everything that is happening in this world, I know that it's difficult to trust God's plan of protection. I am twenty-seven years old, and I can tell you I have been through a lot. When I tell people the things that I have been through, they say, *"You're only in your twenties, and you have been through all of that?"* Yes. And I have SURVIVED through all of that. The enemy has wanted me dead since birth. It is obvious, because he knew I would write this book, and this book would be shown worldwide and expose his plans, encourage others, and break chains. But the fact that I am still here, alive, breathing, and healthy, shows that God is a still a protector.

I can't even count the number of times that God has kept me. He has guarded me from people, places, and situations I had no business being in or around. He has protected me from my family, and He has even had to protect me from *me*.

I grew up in Crown Heights, Brooklyn. I must have been about seven years old; and every night during the summer, I would be out with my family and friends, playing the block until it got dark. We would be back and forth at Lincoln Terrace Park, exposed to things that children had no business being around. Even though I was with friends and family most of the time, sometimes, I traveled alone. I was a tiny pretty girl, with long hair down my back. Any creep could have tried to snatch me up, but God's hand was on me.

When I got a little older, my father put me in modeling school. I went to the Barbizon Modeling Agency where I learned how to walk in heels, walk the runway, do makeup, and all these cute little activities to learn how to be a superstar. I loved it there. I graduated from the school after my final performance, dancing to Beyoncé and walking down the runway. Everybody cheered for me, and I felt like a star. After I graduated, the school offered me a chance to audition for the Disney Channel, but my family didn't have the money at the time, so that was the end of my career at Barbizon.

Every Saturday, I had to get on the train by myself and travel all the way to Manhattan. I really didn't want to travel alone because I was scared, but I had no other choice. My father had already paid for me to go, and I didn't want to disappoint him. I knew how much it meant to him that I would one day be rich and famous, so I got on the E train and attended classes faithfully. Although it was an awesome experience, it was a dangerous mission to travel alone at that age. I can't remember how old I was at the time, but I was fairly young. For my travels, God gave me traveling mercies and protected me in my journey; I remained untouched and unharmed.

Maybe that's nothing to you now but just wait as it gets better…

My father got married and had more kids, and it was time we moved out of my grandmother's house in Brooklyn and got our own space, so we relocated to Flushing, Queens. I was devastated, and I was upset with my father for a long time for moving me out of Brooklyn. I had to leave halfway through the school year while I was in middle school and transfer to Flushing. I graduated from middle school with honors because I was a pretty good student for the most part. Then it was time for me to enter high school.

I attended Jamaica High School, known to be the worst high school in Queens. This school was especially terrifying for freshmen because of the infamous Freshman Friday. There were rumors about how freshmen would get thrown into the pond that was located across the street from our school. We had to go through metal detectors every morning and get our bags searched. I'm not going to lie...this put some fear in my heart. I was thirteen years old, in a completely different borough, and I had no family to protect me. I was in this huge school that looked like a castle, and the kids were double my size. I didn't know how I was going to make it through the schoolyear.

Then here came God in all of His splendor. One of my close friends, Tamera Wills, with whom I had attended middle school and sat with to cheat off all her work, ended up attending the same high school. God gave me a friend so I wouldn't be alone; and not only that, but she had friends and family that were already attending the school. They were juniors and seniors. Oh, I was lit now! I came in as a freshman, and I was hanging with all the seniors. I had NO worries. They taught me everything I needed to know. I got especially close with this boy named Courtney who was a senior, and I had my first crush on him. Yeah, I loved the older guys...they just did it for me.

After they graduated, I was already solidified in high school, so I was able to spread my own wings. Who knew popularity would come with so many haters? I survived Freshman Friday...then I had to survive the Anti-Charline Club! I guess I was just one of those people who females loved to drag my name. There were all kinds of rumors about me floating through the school. I got called all kinds of names behind my back, and God forbid, if a guy liked me that someone else liked...I became number one on their hit list.

For the most part, I had my little crew of girls that I hung out with, and then there were the opposition. Mind you...I'm 4'11," with a loud mouth and a whole lot of attitude. There were girls who wanted my boyfriend, and I was ready to fight anyone who tried to take him. There were girls who wanted to fight me for taking their boyfriend. I wasn't that honors student from middle school anymore, and school was never the same after my sophomore year. It became all about cliques, gossip, drama, and boys.

It never made sense that I was always involved in drama… because I was barely in school! I would come into school during second period to take attendance and leave after third period. If I did manage to stay in school, it would only be up until sixth period, and I was never in my own class—I was either in the hallway or in someone else's class. For some reason, drama couldn't stay too far from me even if I wasn't in the building.

One day after coming into school during third period, I decided I didn't want to go to my class, so I went into my friends' class and stayed there until the bell rang. Class was over; and as soon as I walked out, I looked to the left and saw a mob of girls that I was beefing with at the time walking toward me. All I heard was, *"Charline, take off your jacket. They coming to fight."* I wasn't about to back down, so I took off my jacket and got ready to fight. Everybody was on top of everybody, and the security guards rushed in and broke up the fight. They put me and a few of my friends that jumped in to help in handcuffs. The security guards took us to the office and called the police.

The police said that if they took us in, we were going to have to stay until after the New Year holiday, because the incident took place the day before Thanksgiving, and there were no judges until after the holidays. Now that I'm older and I know better, I'm sure they were trying to scare us; but it worked because I was shook. Luckily, that day God defended me, because they released me and sent me home with a suspension. I wish I could tell you the Lord protected me from the butt whooping I received after that, but unfortunately for me, He didn't. He did give me the strength to endure it though!

God's army of angels was with me all throughout high school. Every day after leaving school, I had to walk down Jamaica Avenue to catch the bus. Jamaica Avenue was violent. No matter the season, someone was always fighting; getting jumped, stabbed, or shot. There were cops everywhere. Surviving the strip wasn't easy. I know, because I used to be the one fighting on the strip and sending hits out on people. Yet every day, I arrived home in one piece. My father had no idea what I was getting myself into or the life that I was living, but he knew it couldn't be anything good. I had a 3:30 pm curfew, but I wasn't making it in the house till around 7:00 or 8:00 pm. I was getting off the bus late at night, and I had to walk through Pomonok Park in the dark to get to my house. As I was walking through the park, I would be singing Jesus Walks by Kanye West; and as I was singing, I knew God was walking with me, and I had no reason to fear. The proof that God is there is that I made it home every night in one piece.

During my senior year, I started partying heavily. I couldn't miss a party. I even had my own dance team, and we would go out and twerk on somebody's son all night. Sometimes, I wouldn't even make it home after a party. When we got old enough to go to the clubs, we turnt all the way up. It was all fun and games until people started fighting and shooting. The crowd I hung out with was not the "Let's study and stay out of trouble" crowd. They were gangbangers, drug dealers, gossipers. They were the ones who loved to fight, had been in the streets, and had real life beef that followed them. Since I was affiliated with them, that meant their problems became my problems.

When we went out, it was always something. I've been to parties where one of my close friends got cracked in the head with a bottle. After leaving another party, myself and a couple of my friends walked outside, and they were letting off shots. One of my friends who was nearby got grazed by a bullet. There was a DJ who was like my brother, and I witnessed him getting hit by a car, which put him in the hospital. His face was dismantled, and his front teeth were cracked. That day was a nightmare, but the Lord was with me, letting no hurt, harm, or danger come near me.

High school really took a toll on me, so I ended up dropping out as a super senior (meaning that I had done my senior year twice) and leaving my parents' house. That's when I gave my life to the streets; and if you didn't think God's hand was on me before, you're going to know that it was now.

I didn't have my own place, so I was moving in with my boyfriends. Most of those relationships ended in terrible domestic violence situations, with me being beaten and choked out. I could have been dead, but God kept me. I was having unprotected sex, but God protected me from HIV/AIDs. When I got pregnant many times and had over six abortions, God covered me and restored my womb.

I was smoking weed and getting belligerently drunk in the clubs, but God kept me by not letting me be raped, violated, or imprisoned. When I was selling hard drugs on the streets, the Lord's angels were with me because I never got pulled over or arrested. When I was driving around in cars that had illegal guns in them, here came the Lord again, keeping me covered and allowing me to make it back home to my son. Thankfully, with everything I was doing and everything going on around me, I never had an Administration for Children's Services case involving my child where he could have been taken away from me.

When I was living in the hardest neighborhoods in New York City and Newark, New Jersey, God gave me too much favor. The people embraced me while I was living there, and God covered me wherever I walked.

God didn't just protect me from people and situations...He also protected me from myself. When I wanted to commit suicide, I took pills and cut my wrists. He kept me. When I started dabbling in New Age spirituality and divination and started losing my mind, God kept me from jumping in front of that car or train. He kept me from flying out of the window after a crash which totaled my car on my way to Atlantic City, when my seatbelt wasn't even working weeks prior. When I did and said things I shouldn't have done or said, I still remember how God saved me from embarrassment; He kept my darkest secrets.

God even protected my family. Nothing will ever compare to the day I was walking home from the supermarket with my son DJ, who was seven at the time. DJ is a very hyperactive child who loves to run around. As we were walking down the sidewalk, he was running ahead of me; and out of nowhere came a car speeding out of a walkway that cars weren't even supposed to be driving through. I was pushing the shopping cart and looking down for cracks on the sidewalk to make sure it didn't tip over, and I happened to look up just in time to see a car speeding toward DJ. I was too far from him to grab him, so I yelled, *"DJ!"* to get his attention. DJ couldn't see the car on the side so instead of running away from the car he ended up running toward it, and literally right before the car hit him, the driver stepped on the brakes, and the car stopped just in time. As a mother, my whole life flashed before my eyes, and my heart was in my throat. I ran to DJ, and my poor baby was so scared. The driver looked at me and apologized. I had every right to curse him out; but grace said, *"Let it go. Comforting your son is more important."* As the driver left, I began to thank God because it could have turned out so much worse.

Some people may still argue and say that's just luck, but what about the things God protected me from that I couldn't see? Who

PROTECTION TESTIMONY

knows what else God has been protecting me from that the enemy was cooking up in the spiritual realm? I'm sure there were plenty of times I was in the wrong place at the wrong time because I didn't have a relationship with God to hear Him tell me where to go and where not to go. I could have been in far worse situations that could have cost me my life.

Let me meet you where you are, and let's be transparent. How many times have you had unprotected sex and God protected you from AIDS or STDs? How many times has He protected you from having a baby with the wrong person after unprotected sex or a one-night stand? How many times has He saved you from those relationships that now, when you look back at them, you say to yourself, *"I don't know what I saw in him/her."* How many times have you thought you were going to die after drinking or smoking too much, and you cried out *"God, if you take this feeling away from me, I will never do it again"* …and you did it again and again. Ladies, how many times have we said, *"Lord, let my period come and I promise, I'll never have sex again."* Fellas, how many times have you gotten caught up and prayed, *"God if you get me out of this situation, I'll never do it again."*

Think about the times He protected you from that stray bullet with your name on it. Think about the times He protected you from the truck you didn't see coming, or that car that you didn't see while you were walking. Or when He protected your children and your family. What about the times He protected you from going insane and killing someone, maybe even your own child? What about the times that person wanted to sexually assault you, but God distracted them by redirecting their attention elsewhere? Think about the times you could have been exposed and God saved you from being humiliated. God is always working even when we don't see Him.

Sometimes, we get spiritual amnesia and forget all that God has protected us from. If you are still here breathing, it's because God

75

has been your protector, your covering, your shield, your rock, your strong tower. We focus so much on what we don't see God doing that we lose sight of everything He has already done.

There are people who argue that if God protects them then why is He letting innocent babies be killed and letting people do this or that? Why is there all of this madness going on in the world? I wish I knew how to answer this question for you; but unfortunately, God is too big to understand exactly why He allows some things to happen. What I do know is that when we allow sin into our lives, we give the enemy access to destroy our homes and our families.

When we choose to serve the devil, we give him permission to wreak havoc in our lives. The Bible says in ***John 10:10*** that the thief comes *"to kill, to steal, and to destroy."* You can't give a thief keys to your house and expect him not to take everything in it…that's who he is! There are bad things that happen to good people; it rains on the just and the unjust. I even questioned God about why He took certain people out of my life. As I got older, God allowed me to understand that if this didn't happen, this wouldn't have happened, for me to be here, and have this.

God does everything for a reason, and He makes no mistakes. He never said the weapons wouldn't form…He said they wouldn't *prosper*. Bad things may have happened in your life, but through it, you may have learned something valuable; it may have strengthened you, or it may have been the very testimony God needed for you to help someone else one day. God still is sovereign at the end of the day, and His promises still stand. He promises to defend and protect us. He promises to keep us safe from hidden dangers and deadly diseases. He promises to remove all fear from us. He promises that no matter what is happening around us, it will not come near us. He promises that no disaster or violence will come near us. He promises to assign angels to our lives to protect us wherever we go, and He promises that when we call on Him, He will answer us and rescue us, because He has given us authority over the devil and his wicked schemes.

I advise you to close the door and change the locks on the enemy. Follow Christ and you too will see the promises of God. It helps to build a relationship with the Holy Spirit so He will give you the discernment to know good from bad and right from wrong. Read His Word so you will know His voice, so that when the time comes, you will hear Him tell you to be still or don't go there and know when He gives you the permission to do something.

I'm not in the convincing business. I'm not here to make anyone believe that God is who He says He is. It is only when you believe that you can receive, and I can only testify because I have overcome death many times, both when I was aware and unaware. I speak only of the goodness of God because I wouldn't be here today if it wasn't for Him.

DIVINE PROTECTION

"If you say, 'The Lord is my refuge,' and you make the Most High your dwelling, no harm will overtake you, no disaster will come near your tent. For he will command his angels concerning you to guard you in all your ways."
(Psalm 91:9-11 NIV)

JEHOVAH MAGEN *(GENESIS 15:1)*

The name of the Lord is a strong tower, the righteous run to it and are safe. My soul waits for you, you are my help and my shield. My heart is glad in you because I trust your holy name. I praise you for your steadfast love as I put my hope in you. There is no one on earth who can protect me better than you can. I magnify you for being my shield against the fiery darts of the enemy. I sing for joy as you spread your protection over me, for those who love your name may rejoice in you. I bow before the name of Jehovah Magen. I thank you, for you are my great reward.

Forgive me if I have sinned against you, forcing you to remove your hedge of protection from around me. Forgive me if I have tested your ability to protect me from my own ungodly behaviors. I understand that your desire is for me to be safe, though I live in a fallen world. I trust in you to cover me from the harm of outsiders intending to cause anguish that results in unexpected accidents, mishaps, or tragedies. Scripture says, *"Ask and it will be given unto you, seek and you will find" (**Matthew 7:7 NIV**)*. This includes the protection of God; therefore, I ask for your covering against unseen dangers, in Jesus' name.

As I rest in your shadow and live in your spiritual shelter, assign your angels to cover the windows and doors of my home from trespassers and intruders. I place your blood on my doorpost as a sign that my home is marked, commanding the angel of death to pass over. As I travel to and from my destinations, send your traveling mercies to be with me. Place your hedge of thorns in front of me when I am approaching danger zones. Grant me the discernment to realize when disaster is near and redirect my path. Your Word is a lamp for my feet, a light for my path. Place me on the right path that will sustain your safeguarding.

Lord, my only safe place is you. Sometimes, I can be my own worst enemy, so protect me from causing destruction to myself. Guard my mind, my body, and my soul, so that the mindset on the flesh would be sentenced to death but my mind on the spirit will live. Make it impossible for me to participate in activities that will wreck my spirit. Holy Spirit, convict me when I am engaging in wrongful behavior and redirect my mind to you. I put on the full armor of God according to **Ephesians 6:10-18**. I put on the helmet of salvation, the breastplate of righteousness, the belt of truth. I put on the shoes of peace and preparation. I take up the shield of faith and the sword of the spirit, which is the Word of God. As I take my stand against the wiles of the enemy, let no weapons formed against me prosper and condemn every tongue that rises up against me, in the name of Jesus.

I decree **Psalm 91** over my life. Lord, I am trusting you to keep me safe as I take cover under your feathers. Remember your promise to deliver me from the snare of the fowler and from the noisome pestilence. That I shall not be afraid of the terror by night nor the arrow that flies by day, though a thousand may fall at my side, ten thousand at my right hand, it will not come near me. You promise that no harm can overtake me, and no disaster can come near me. Your angels shall lift me up, so that I will not strike my foot against a stone. You have given me the authority to tread on the lion and the cobra, to trample on the great lion and the serpent. Your Word is sharper than a double-edged sword, cutting through bone and marrow, and I believe that it will not return to me void, in Jesus' name.

Father, my only safe place is in you. Thank you for encompassing me with your strength and your might. Thank you for covering me from injury, catastrophe, or calamity. Thank you for sending your angels to war on my behalf. Thank you for keeping me from both the seen and unseen dangers of the world, danger from people, and even my personal spiritual danger. Thank you for delivering me from all my troubles. Thank you for your precious blood.

I decree that I will keep my eyes always on the Lord; with Him at my right hand, I will not be shaken. I decree when I pass through the rivers, they will not sweep over me; when I walk through the fire, I will not be burned; the flames will not set me ablaze. I decree and declare *"The God of my strength, in whom I trust; my shield and the horn of my salvation, my stronghold and my refuge; my Savior, you save me from violence" (**2 Samuel 22:3 NASB**).*

I seal this declaration in the blood of the Lamb, and I pray all of this in the matchless name of Jesus. Amen.

PROTECTION OVER FAMILY

"'Because he loves me,' says the Lord, 'I will rescue him; I will protect him, for he acknowledges my name. He will call on me, and I will answer him; I will be with him in trouble, I will deliver him and honor him.'"
(Psalm 91:14-15 NIV)

JEHOVAH SABAOTH *(1 SAMUEL 1:3)*

You are the Lord of Armies. I thank you for your army of angels that are warring and fighting for us every day. Blessed be your name, the Lord of Hosts, who is omnipotent and sovereign. I will praise you and tell everyone that you are my hiding place. I glory in you, my God who is always on duty fighting those who fight against your beloved. For this cause, I bow my knee unto the Father of our Lord Jesus Christ.

Father, may I remind you of your promise…you do not wish for anyone to perish but for everyone to come to repentance. As I intercede on behalf of my family, I pray that those who are not yet believers will begin seeking salvation and turn from their wicked ways, repent, and humble themselves, so that you may forgive their sins. I pray that my family will commit to the works of the Lord and begin to hunger and thirst after righteousness. There is no one too far from your reach, and there is nothing dead that you cannot resurrect. Reach out your mighty hand and arrest their hearts, drawing them back to you.

I repent on behalf on my bloodline. I pray that you forgive my family members of their shortcomings, their rebellion, and their stubborn ways. Forgive the generation whose hearts were not loyal to you and whose spirits were not faithful. Renew their hearts and put a burden on them to release any unforgiveness they may be harboring, so that we may be unified as one. I pray that your love, mercy, and grace will cover their sins, in the name of Jesus.

I acknowledge that many family members are going through oppression, betraying and killing each other. I speak against division, tension, strife, bitterness, rage, murder, destruction, calamity, or chaos, from the plots, ploys, or plans of the enemy. I cancel every plan from the enemy that tries to unravel peace in my home or my family's lives. Satan, I send you a heavenly eviction notice; you must depart from my bloodline and never return, in the name of Jesus.

Lord, **Proverbs 4:6** says, *"Do not forsake wisdom, and she will protect you; love her, and she will watch over you."* According to your Word, I ask that you grant my family the wisdom and discernment to steer away from the wiles of the enemy. Keep your children safe from the hands of the wicked; protect them from the violent, who devise ways to trip our feet. Although the weapons may form, they will not prosper. Make my family bulletproof against the ambush of the enemy. I lift up my eyes to the hills from where my help will come. My help comes from the Lord. Help me be the intercessor that my family needs to keep them from walking into danger.

Lord, do not withhold your mercy. Cover and protect your

children in their homes, outside their homes, at school, at work, in their car, in the courtrooms, and wherever else their feet may walk. Cover their minds, bodies, souls, and spirits. Break every yoke of the enemy off of my bloodline. Break every curse that was placed on my family to cause destruction. Release a heavenly blood transfusion through my bloodline. Call forth the men and women of valor in my bloodline who are called by your name and chosen for such a time as this. Put the right people in their path, those who have a love for the Lord, to encourage them as they delight themselves in you. Let them have a special encounter with you as you shield them from all hurt, harm, or danger. Let your love, power, and a sound mind be their portion, in the name of Jesus.

Thank you for not being slow in keeping your promises. Thank you for keeping my family as the apple of your eye, hiding them under the shadow of your wings. Thank you for being near to the brokenhearted and crushed in spirit. Thank you for delivering your righteous from affliction.

I decree the name of the LORD is a strong tower; the righteous run to it and are safe. I decree the LORD is a helper; my family will not fear. I decree that I will be still as you fight for my family. I decree and declare that my family will be saved, sustained, and rescued. I decree and declare that if God is for us, nothing can be against us.

I seal this declaration in the blood of the Lamb, and I pray all of this in the matchless name of Jesus. Amen.

PROTECTION OVER THE NATIONS

"I urge, then, first of all, that petitions, prayers, intercession and thanksgiving be made for all people for kings and all those in authority, that we may live peaceful and quiet lives in all godliness and holiness. This is good, and pleases God our Savior, who wants all people to be saved and to come to a knowledge of the truth."
(1 Timothy 2:1-4 NIV)

JEHOVAH NISSI *(EXODUS 15:16-17)*

Hallowed be your name. Your kingdom come, your will be done, on earth as it is in heaven. Thank you for the men and women who serve our country. You have given me a mandate to pray for everyone who is in authority. The world that you created has turned into a fallen one, filled with sin because your children have turned away from you. Lord, I lift up the nations to you. Pour out your spirit. Send the power of the prophet Elijah to turn the hearts of your people back to you. Bless the land so we will no longer be a goat nation but a sheep nation who will follow our good shepherd.

Lord, protect the nation from all government attacks, terrorist attacks, all forms of mass destruction, chemical and biological warfare, drug trafficking, sex trafficking, racism, gun violence, bombings, suicide attacks, rocket and mortar attacks, vehicular attacks, aircraft and hijacking attacks, nuclear weapons, cyberterrorism, radiation poisoning, secondary attacks, and all other forms of warfare that target our nation, in the name of Jesus.

You are a patient God who keeps His promises, not wanting anyone to perish but everyone to come to repentance. I stand in the gap on behalf of the nation, putting a demand on you to heal the land. I pray that your people who are in positions of authority and those who are called by your name will humble themselves and pray, seek your face, and turn from their wicked ways, so you may forgive their sins and heal the nations.

> **Python spirits:** spirits that squeeze the life out of you, leaving you unhappy and depressed.

I bind up and destroy every spirit in the nation that manifests idol worship, sex trafficking, child pornography, domestic violence, poverty, mass destruction, python spirits, terrorist attacks, fear, warfare, racism, and death, in the mighty name of Jesus. Heal this land from pain, immorality, confusion, wickedness, pride, rebellion, rejection, and depression. Cure the sickness and disease that is causing the nations' citizens to fear. I prophesy that those who don't know you will begin to know you and love you with all their heart, soul, and mind. Send hope to your people and show them that there is eternal life awaiting them, in the name of Jesus.

I pray for our president, government leaders, officers, state officials, political leaders, those who are serving in office, serving in the churches, and the families of those who serve in authority. I lift them up to you so you can touch their lives and release harmony and unity into their homes. Teach them how to balance their work and family lives. Give their spouses patience and give their children peace in the midst of troubling times. Send your angels to guard them and protect their homes from any danger or acts of evil against them due to their positions in authority.

Lord, give to all the men and women who serve this country your supernatural strength and stamina to endure long hours in the office and on the field. Relieve them from their stress, and grant them the peace that transcends all understanding, along with prosperity in their work lives. Teach them how to steward their power well, and send them godly connections who will support, encourage, and pray for them. One could chase a thousand, but two could put ten thousand to flight. Teach those whose hearts desire change to unify with other believers to pray for the land. Give them ears to listen to your divine instruction that will fulfill your perfect will for our nation. Give them godly wisdom for political change and problem-solving decrees. Guide their steps and lead them as they lead. Store up your commandments in their hearts, giving them insight and foresight as they cry out for understanding. Help them to understand the fear of the Lord, and find the knowledge of you, so that they will sin no more, in Jesus' name.

Give your leaders a heart of flesh and fill their hearts with kindness to be tenderhearted and vulnerable to the needs of your people. Teach them how to show proper respect to everyone, love the family of believers, honor those in authority, and serve the Lord with fear.

Send your spirit to fill their hearts with love and reverence for you. Guide their conversations that will lead to breakthroughs for our country. Shield them in your mercy, grace, and love, teaching them how to discipline the nations, not with a heart of stone but with a heart of flesh. Give them divine systems, strategies, and structures to end poverty. Shield the nations' leaders with courage to boldly face evil and move into action. Bless the work of their hands to write new laws that will divinely bless your people, in Jesus' name.

I acknowledge that everyone is subject to the governing authorities that exist and have been established by God. You have the power and authority to make nations great and destroy them, enlarge the nations and disperse them, deprive the leaders and make them wander in a trackless waste. Remove all those in authority who are not pleasing to you. Remove those who are causing pain to the land. I pray that celebrities will begin to come forth and turn from their wicked ways. I pray they will begin to use their platforms to influence and encourage the nations.

In Jesus' name, I pray those leaders and influencers with an abundance of wealth would begin to use their money and wealth to change the communities and help end poverty. Raise up the leader and send out the evangelist. Raise up those who are called to run for office. Raise up the entrepreneurs who will create jobs that will end poverty. Raise up leaders who will be more involved in their communities and make a difference. Teach the influencers how to influence the nations using your prophetic stream of gifts and talents. Teach them how to influence the masses using platforms such as social media, art, music, dancing, the internet, and more.

Lord, you hold the success of the nations, and you give it to those whose walk is upright and blameless. You said that if you could find a few righteous in the nations that for the sake of the righteous, you will spare the nations. Protect the way of your faithful ones. I seek peace and prosperity for the nation because if it prospers, so will we prosper. You looked for someone among them who will stand in the gap on behalf of the land so you will not destroy it, and I say, *"Here I am, Lord. Send me."* With your guidance, I decree and declare the nation will not fall because victory is won, in Jesus' name.

I seal this declaration in the blood of the Lamb, and I pray all of this in the matchless name of Jesus. Amen.

PROTECTION FROM ILLNESSES AND DISEASES

"I will say of the Lord, 'He is my refuge and my fortress, my God, in whom I trust.' Surely, he will save you from the fowler's snare and from the deadly pestilence."
(Psalm 91:2-3 NIV)

ADONAI TZEVAOT *(JOSHUA 5:13)*

I bless the name of Adonai Tzevaot. I praise you for being my strong tower. I trust in you, my refuge and my fortress, to cover me against any and all sickness and disease. You treasure your children, not wanting any harm to come their way. I hold on to you as my security blanket, and I make you my place of habitation. I trust in you to protect me against any deadly pestilence. I lift up your name; your praises will forever be on my lips, as I glorify in you for being my shield and my buckler. I praise you because although millions of people are dying daily, you keep me and breathe life into my lungs.

Father, forgive me for the sins that allowed the enemy access to my body. Please don't strike me with sickness, disease, illness, flu, fever, inflammation, or infection. Don't let the evil works of the enemy pursue me. You sent your only Son to destroy the works of the devil, letting no one snatch me out of your hand. I believe in your power to shelter me from any deadly pestilence.

Lord, I cannot survive without you. I live in a fallen world where there are outbreaks of disease. Send your spirit to place an order of protection over me during contagious widespread infections. Grant me a divine immune system that will withstand global epidemics. As I meditate on your promises, I trust that your Word will not return unto me void.

In my temple is where your Holy Spirit dwells. I pray for protection against all bacteria and germs that could cause any harm to me physically, mentally, emotionally, or spiritually. Send your angels to encamp around me, and guard myself and my family from illness. As I rest in you, remove all anxiety, worry, and stress that weakens my immune system. Bring health and healing to the areas in my life that have opened the doors to poor health, and close the doors to any future health problems, in the name of Jesus.

Lord, you are faithful, and you will not tempt me more than I can bear. Grant me the discipline to be a good steward over my body and respect myself enough to not consume anything that will cause infirmities to manifest. Guard me from the sickness and disease that comes from smoking or consumption of alcohol. You have called me for great works for which I must be healthy to prosper in the things of God to serve you with excellence. Grant me a full and complete life span to carry out your assignment. Keep me from my own selfish desires that may cause evil to my body. Watch over my life, and protect me from unseen infections. Provide me with peace and hope in the middle of despair.

Shine your light on any areas in my life that need repentance so that I may be in right standing with you. Help me to keep your commandments so there will be no open doors for any malady.

Lord, I know that my life is precious to you. The Word of God says, *"If you will diligently listen to the voice of the Lord your God, and do that which is right in his eyes, and give ear to his commandments and keep all his statutes, I will put none of the diseases on you that I put on the Egyptians, for I am the Lord, your healer"* **(Exodus 15:26 NIV)**. Thank you for keeping me from disease. Thank you, for I have no reason to fear or panic because your faithfulness is my shield and my rampart. Thank you for combatting my afflictions before they even begin. Thank you for your love that covers me under your wings. Thank you for covering me that I may have peace and security. I thank you for your sacrifice on the Cross that took my illness and bore my diseases; because you shed your blood, it is declared finished. I decree and declare that no evil shall befall me; no plague will come near my tent. I decree and declare that though a thousand may fall at my side, ten thousand at my right hand, it will not come near me. I decree and declare that I am secure in Christ and will not lose heart. I decree and declare that I am walking in divine protection.

I seal this declaration in the blood of the Lamb, and I pray all of this in the matchless name of Jesus. Amen.

THE SINNER'S PRAYER...

If you have never accepted the Lord Jesus into your heart, I invite you to do so here, with me.

Father, I confess that I am a sinner, and that without the saving work of your Son on the Cross, I am destined for the fires of hell. I confess my sins to you now and ask you to enter my heart and cleanse me, leaving me white as snow. I believe that God raised Jesus from the dead according to **Romans 8:11**. *Lord, I believe that you are the Way, the Truth, and the Life, and I ask you to take me as I am, and make me new. Today, I confess with my mouth and believe in my heart that Jesus Christ is my Lord and Savior. I declare that I am reborn. I am a Christian. I am a child of God. I am* **Saved**.

In the precious name of Jesus, I pray. Amen.

ABOUT THE AUTHOR

CHARLINE AYALA is an author, entrepreneur, intercessor, and mother. She is the CEO of Charline Ayala Enterprises LLC and Kingdom Kids Collection.

As a victim of domestic violence, Charline has a dream to create Women in Control (W.I.C.) to help women take back their authority and dominion and fix the crown of glory that God has given them. She also dreams of starting the Reverse the Curse Outreach, because with the heavy generational curse of witchcraft and black magic running through her bloodline, she fell into the trap of the enemy, making agreements with Satan.

She started Charline Ayala Enterprises and Kingdom Kids Collection to break poverty off of her bloodline, create generational wealth, and to be a beacon for the Lord through evangelism, while spreading the good news and raising up a generation of children to do the same.

With all that she has accomplished, she's most proud of serving her Abba Father and allowing Him to use her in a mighty way.

Charline was born in Brooklyn, NY and was raised in Brooklyn and Queens. She is the oldest of her five siblings and mother to her one and only son, DJ Kelly Jr.

Charline gave her life to Christ in August of 2019 and was baptized on October 13th of the same year. She joined D3 Ministries, where she completed her discipleship classes and began her walk with Christ. Charline is now on a mission to preach fire to the nations; and with her gift of leadership, she aims to bring as many souls as she can to Christ before His kingdom comes and His will be done. Now, she and her son are walking in ministry together; delivering, empowering, and developing the nations to give God all the glory.

ACKNOWLEDGMENTS

I want to thank my wonderful pastors, **Marcel** and **Ruth Langhorn,** for the love that you have given me since I joined D3 Ministries. My life has never been the same, and I thank you for allowing God to use you in developing me into the woman I am today.

Thank you to my best friends, **Christina Davis** and **Junior Marcel,** for supporting me through this journey. I know it's not easy loving me, but I thank the Lord for the strength that He has given you to stay by my side. Thank you for always being my ear to listen and my shoulder to cry on.

Thank you to **Mike** and **Kelly Logan** for the creative direction for this book and for the wisdom and counsel that you have given me to help make my vision come alive.

REFERENCES

https://www.openbible.info
https://www.biblestudytools.com
https://www.womansday.com
https://www.bibliatodo.com/en/names-of-God/
https://www.embracingasimplerlife.com/
https://wealthanize.com/bible-prosperity-scriptures/
https://www.christian-faith.com/
https://www.biblegateway.com
https://walkinlove.com
https://www.crosswalk.com
https://christianstt.com
https://www.ministrymaker.com
https://www.enlivenpublishing.com
https://www.christianity.com
https://bible.knowing-jesus.com
https://www.worldvision.org

CONTACT INFORMATION

If you would like to contact the author directly, you may do so at *AuthorCharlineAyala@gmail.com*

Instagram
@Endtimewarrior_

Facebook
Charline Ayala

Website
Charlineayala.com

www.ingramcontent.com/pod-product-compliance
Lightning Source LLC
Chambersburg PA
CBHW051452290426
44109CB00016B/1730